Walking in God's Grace ~~is ... .~~
overlook — God's grace is not only essential to entering the Christian life, it is also essential for living it. Through a careful handling of Scripture, the exciting truth is stressed that victory in the Christian life comes not from focusing on the promises we have made to Him, but the provision He has made for us on the cross. Any believer who wants to know how the grace of God applies to the here and now will be helped by reading this book.
Dr. R. Larry Moyer, Founder & CEO, EvanTell

In their new guidebook, *Walking in God's Grace: Practical Answers to Tough Questions,* World Prayr has created a much needed resource for believers — baby and bustling alike. Through an exhaustive list of questions and well-crafted answers meant to challenge and grow followers of Messiah, the book educates and strengthens both readers and inquirers. Topics include grace, sin, forgiveness, relating to family, the promises of life in Jesus, obedience, church and even discerning God's will. While not claiming to be a theological treatise, the answers are Bible-centered and very practical. Readers will be drawn to dig deeper into the Scriptures as they make their way through this thought-provoking book.

In addition to the paper product, World Prayr provides an expanded resources section with other books, periodicals, blogs, podcasts and online message repositories, as well as material from the authors themselves.

My colleague at Jews for Jesus, Sean Trank, has long appreciated the unique online ministry of World Prayr as they provide a great service to believers by highlighting needs and fostering prayer globally. World Prayr, through this new publication, will add a great resource for our online network of volunteers who are often asked to answer difficult questions. We now have another valuable tool to add to our arsenal of answers.
Susan Perlman, Associate Executive Director, Jews for Jesus

A needed return to grace-empowered living that will establish new Christians in biblical thinking and struggling Christians in biblical freedom and joy.

This book delivers grace-based living through a return to foundational truths of holiness and sin that makes grace the rich biblical truth that it is.

New Christians will be glad for a resource that develops them by answering the questions that challenge their faith. Established Christians will be grateful for a resource that guides them in their spiritual conversations with those whom they disciple.
Pastor Mike Haury, Crossroads Community Church, Madison Ohio

For those who have never experienced God's grace, and for those who have not yet discovered that their own righteousness is woefully inadequate, this book provides a practical guide for living a joyful Christian life, filled with God's grace. Its pages are filled with God's extravagant love for mankind as well as admonition for avoiding the trap of legalism. It clearly points out the distinction between law and grace and the role of each in our walk with the Lord.

The question and answer format makes it easy to find specific information, such as how to study the Bible or pray. Especially helpful is the fact that in most cases scripture references are quoted rather that depending on the reader to look them up in their Bible. Caution is given to those who read passages in isolation and base their beliefs on less than the entire Bible.

The pages of this book will expand your horizons and provoke thoughtful self examination.

Wendell Rovenstine, Executive Vice President, Voice of China and Asia

In *Walking in God's Grace – Practical Answers to Tough Questions* World Prayr have tackled a topic that many writers shy away from because it is not possible to teach "grace" as it should be, without appearing to some, to sanction licentious living. But let God be God! In reality, the challenge most of have as believers, is the problem of the journey from heart to head. Our hearts know that we are saved by grace because that's where salvation takes place. However, as human beings, our heads somehow find it difficult to accept the truth that we can be justified and sanctified without us doing anything.

In *Walking in God's Grace* World Prayr have succeeded in showing in practical ways, how we can get our heads to understand and accept what our hearts already know: the fact that in the words of Brennan Manning in *All Is Grace: A Ragamuffin Memoir* "God loves you unconditionally, as you are and not as you should be, because nobody is as they should be. It is the message of grace…A grace that pays the eager beaver who works all day long the same wages as the grinning drunk who shows up at ten till five…. A grace that hikes up the robe and runs breakneck toward the prodigal reeking of sin and wraps him up and decides to throw a party no ifs, ands, or buts…. This grace is indiscriminate compassion. It works without asking anything of us…. Grace is sufficient even though we huff and puff with all our might to try to find something or someone it cannot cover. Grace is enough…. Jesus is enough."

Walking in God's Grace provides to the point answers to difficult questions about the meaning and scope of grace, as well as our response to God in the face of His unconditional love. It is well written and easy to read. I believe it will be blessing to the Body of Christ.

Dr. Pedro Okoro
Lead Pastor, New Covenant Church, Wallington, Surrey, UK
author of *Crushing the Devil*

WALKING IN GOD'S GRACE

PRACTICAL ANSWERS TO TOUGH QUESTIONS

World Prayr

Energion Publications
Gonzalez, FL
2014

ISBN10: 1-63199-025-X
ISBN13: 978-1-63199-025-0
Library of Congress Control Number: 2014950989

World Prayr
info@worldprayr.org

Energion Publications
energion.com

ACKNOWLEDGMENTS

We take this opportunity not only to thank those who have worked so hard on this book but those who inspire us constantly by their service, dedication, friendship, and lives honoring the Father. These are true "Difference Makers" and in a minute we will tell you how we describe that term.

First to God the Father, Jesus the Son, and the Holy Spirit to whom we owe our very lives. Thank You for the plan that You put into place long before You created the world. You made us Your children and bride through Your grace.

To those who take the time to read this and put in the hard work, we pray it will be a very valuable resource for you.

To those we have had the privilege of serving, from individuals to ministries to churches, thank you for allowing us to worship God by serving you and living Philippians 2:2-4 and Romans 12:10.

To Pat Badstibner, the founder of World Prayr, for compiling the material for this book. Like many before him, he has a passion for souls to be received into God's Kingdom.

To Henry and Jody Neufeld of Energion Publications thank you for being our partners in ministry, our friends, and for the support and hard work to publish what we hope will be a very valuable resource.

To our Board and Senior Teams as a whole, thank you for the tireless work and efforts you continually give, the support, direction, spiritual guidance, friendship, leadership and heart work.

To those bloggers and podcasters who provide us with content and allow us to share your thoughts on God's Word, we are blessed and touched by the lives you are touching.

To our team in general, thank you for making God's work happen by being Kingdom-minded and serving others.

To those individuals who make this ministry happen through their tireless efforts, service, heart-driven hard work, dedication, and diligence. They provide examples of what it means to be a true "Servant of the Most High God." They are scattered all over the world and yet we are blessed to serve together. So thank you: Alan, Alice, Andria, Becky, Bernard, Bob, Brenda, Calvin, Catherine, Charlie, Christi, Darren, David, Ebony, Elsie, Erik, Feni, Gabby, Gilbert, Henry, Howard, James, Janice, Jason, Javier, Jessica, Joanne, John, John, Katherine, Lenir, Leroy, Libby, Lindy, Lynda, Mark, Marlynn, Maxwell, Mic. Pete, Portia, Rishie, Robert, Royaelty, Ruth, Santi, Steve, Tatiana, Theodora, Tom, Waheed, Wini, Yohana and their families who also serve by their support and sacrifice. We call them our **Difference Makers**.

A Difference Maker dares to see things differently. They do so because they realize Jesus Christ has given them the freedom to do so. They choose not to just focus on what separates them but what joins them. It is the commonality in the belief that they are more alike than they are different. This likeness brings them to realize that what once separated them now brings them together or it should, can and will. In coming together for the greater good, they realize their differences are defined from others. The recognition of that difference not only creates a deep gratitude but a deep sorrow as well. Both the gratitude and the sorrow push them to greater heights, deeper challenges, bigger risks and a focused vision. The vision of a Difference Maker sees the commonality which can lead to a desire to do things differently in order to become rebels, radical, wild, and out of order. In fact they welcome such labels.

Jesus himself was considered to be truly different and unique and so his followers work, live, worship, and serve as examples to others who in turn realize they too have been called to be different.

TABLE OF CONTENTS

INTRODUCTION

Perhaps you have just accepted Christ as your Savior or maybe you have been saved for a while and just have some questions or are looking for answers to some questions. We may not have covered all your questions in our book, nor all the answers. It is only our intention to help you grow further in your journey.

In 1964 a rock and roll band, *The Animals*, recorded a narrative song that would be a number one hit and become a cult classic, *The House of the Rising Sun*. In the song, the soloist speaks of life wasted in sin and misery. As he pleads with mothers to not let their children go down to *The House of the Rising Sun*, he points out "many a poor boy" has lost his life there and he sadly admits, "I'm one."

In 1895 William Newell, a Bible teacher at Moody Bible Institute, also reflected on a troubled youth. Newell penned his testimony to prose and that prose became the beautiful hymn we know today as *At Calvary*. Two songs describing the two aspects of grace. Without understanding the first song and accepting we are indeed "one wasted in sin and misery," we cannot appreciate the beauty of the hope in the second song.

This is where confusion lies, discourse occurs, mistakes happen, and lives falter. We do not have the vocabulary to express the reality of our condition without God's atoning grace. As a result we fail to see the gospel as good enough.

It is not that we are just broken. Rather it is as if all the kings' horses and all the kings' men were to look upon **us**, and decide to rescue Humpty Dumpty first! If we look upon our good deeds, those works we think we do so well, through the eyes of God (after all, His opinion is what matters, right?) we would surely rather handle a live skunk.

We are not OK. In fact we are in need of a desperate heart transplant. The only problem is, the hearts available are all dead in sin, like ours.

We are condemned to spend eternity with our own vices, thoughts, interests, senses and inspections. C. S. Lewis in his great book *The Great Divorce* said, "I do not think that all who choose wrong roads perish; but their rescue consists in being put back on the right road."

This is our fate, our destiny. Because one of us screwed up, the rest are forever tied to the railroad tracks of condemnation with the train of eternity just seconds away. Not to mention we are hopeless, and absolutely powerless, to do anything to rescue ourselves. No, we are indeed in desperate need of a rescue, of a Savior.

Hell is indeed real. It is a place of torment and separation from our Creator. We wander with unquenchable thirst, completely lost in our own devices. Unless mercy is given, pardon is multiplied and grace is free, we will be forever lost.

Dante, in his *Inferno*, pens the following quotes to describe Hell:

> "Through me you go into a city of weeping; through me you go into eternal pain; through me you go amongst the lost people" and

> "Ye who enter, abandon all hope."

Jesus, the perfect God-man, had a vision as He prayed in the Garden of Gethsemane. He saw what we humans face on our own. Without Jesus' perfect sacrifice, our self-formed destiny leads straight to the wrath of God, and that scene shook Him to the core. For the first time He knew fear, He knew emotional torment to such a degree His sweat became like drops of blood. The sin that exists in all of us demanded that because of God's justice we suffer hell. Instead, Christ suffered on the cross what we deserved, not because He deserved it but because we did.

That is why the cross exists and is the greatest sign of God's passionate love towards His creation. The cross does not exist because there was any value in us, or we have, or could ever have something to offer.

We do not get, keep, sustain, maintain or receive this gift because we have confessed all of our sins and somehow became worthy of this gift. We never will and never could. The psalmist said in Psalm 130:3, "If you O LORD, should mark iniquities, LORD, who could stand?" (ESV) The writer of the psalm realizes he also could never atone for his sins. God's great love, and only His love for us, creates the way to Jesus and redeems us from deserved punishment.

If this was a fairy tale, we are not the heroine like Sleeping Beauty, Cinderella, or even Belle. We are something even more despicable than the evil queen.

No! We are indeed the **Beast!** Our only value is the value instilled by the Creator. Yet, the Creator does not just place and find value in us. He desires us, runs after us, chooses us and redeems us unto **Himself** so we might be His chosen bride.

We have been wallowing in the pigsty, while **He** has been preparing for the ultimate party, the most lavish of weddings – **ours**! Now **He** has called us in, awaits to eagerly lavish abounding, everlasting **grace** to us and give us freedom to love **Him** back.

He is shouting as He offers His grace to us, not "How To's" or "Steps To" but an "**It is finished.**" Yet we refuse to accept it, believing in our arrogance and pride that God must allow us do something.

This is not our story, but God's. A love story and a story of redemption. As God chases His beloved, US, to redeem them to Himself. Not because of what we do, could do or will do but because of what He did.

The record books have been closed as a result of Christ saying "It Is Finished." Christ gave the ultimate performance, the one we could never give and there are no further applications being accepted by God for the performance of a lifetime. God promised before the foundations of the world that He had a plan; Christ was the fulfillment of that plan. The perfect one became our sin because only He could and as a result God has promised life eternally to all those who now place their faith in that perfect sacrifice.

Now God is not calling us to a life of greater performance, to pick ourselves up so we can do more, be more or accomplish more. For all that needed to be done has been done, and what needed to be accomplished was. He has freed those He calls His own to be able to become what they were originally designed to be.

It really is a worthwhile question to ponder, reflect on and answer, "What are you going to do with your new found freedom?" Knowing our deep need for the ugliness of the cross and God's great love towards us should compel us to worship God and serve others, which was Paul's reasoning behind his plea in his letter to the Romans:

> So here's what I want you to do, God helping you: Take your everyday, ordinary life—your sleeping, eating, going-to-work, and walking-around life—and place it before God as an offering. Embracing what God does for you is the best thing you can do for him. Don't become so well-adjusted to your culture that you fit into it without even thinking. Instead, fix your attention on God. You'll be changed from the inside out. Readily recognize what he wants from you, and quickly respond to it. Unlike the culture around you, always dragging you down to its level of immaturity, God brings the best out of you, develops well-formed maturity in you. (Romans 12:1-2, The Message)

Through our obedience we no longer say, "Please approve of me" but "I love You" to the One who calls us in spite of ourselves, **His** beloved. Then when we abuse, misuse, waste, and trash His grace, as well as rebel, disobey and just flat out blow it, He responds with "I understand you're human, but I am the I AM. Remember you love Me because I am absolutely **crazy** about you." That is the message of God's love, called grace and where our journey begins as we learn "how to walk in that grace" through the questions and answers of this book.

It was not our intention to provide theological discourse, but practical, Biblical answers. Imagine yourself having a chat with a friend over a cup of coffee or tea at a table about what it means to"Live in Grace." We may even repeat ourselves, Heaven forbid, in some of our answers. Each question was treated as a completely separate question, apart from the rest, so that if someone is asking a particular question, they have a complete answer available. Our hope is that this serves as a valuable resource, providing to the point answers to some tough questions.

The answers may even seem incomplete; perhaps we have done that for a reason. Remember these are table top answers and often one in a table top conversation only has enough time to give a quick answer.

There may be questions that should have been included, so some would feel. Volumes have been written on most of these questions. We recognize we just barely skim the surface because "we are foolish half-hearted creatures, much more content to play with mud pies" (paraphrased from *The Weight of Glory* by C. S. Lewis).

Our answers may be attacked by greater minds than ours for not being critical enough, deep enough, thoughtful enough, correct enough or even scriptural enough. Yet, these are the answers we often give when asked these very questions. At the end of the booklet, we include a resource section with a list of books, blogs, podcasts and authors that we recommend. We encourage you to dig deeper into these resources as you move further on your journey.

We pray that this would not serve as the be all and end all, but rather the beginning of discourse, thought, discussion and inspiration to seek out deeper, better, more qualified answers as you walk this journey. For it is God's desire that you not only help increase your own personal faith but also be prepared to have an answer for every man that asks you about the hope you have in Christ (1 Peter 3:15).

Do not be surprised to find that our answers do not suffice or contradict what you see in Scripture. We are OK with that. Author Brennan Manning once said we are "only pilgrims who may or may not have answers to give and who may or may not be further ahead, for we are only pilgrims, just like you."

We close this introduction with a refrain from William Newell's beautiful hymn. And if you find you have further questions, please feel free to contact us at info@worldprayr.org.

> Mercy there was great, and grace was free;
> Pardon there was multiplied to me;
> There my burdened soul found liberty, at Calvary.

Questions and Answers

What is Grace?

God has many qualities and gifts, but of all **His qualities** none express **His character** or does He have a **better gift** than **His grace.** All grace originates with God. Grace can be classified into two main categories. These categories are often classified as common grace and special or what we might refer to as transforming, saving grace. Common grace is that which everyone experiences whether they believe in it or not. Common grace is not relevant to us placing faith in it or even believing in God to experience it. It is God at work in the very world around us as we live in our day to day lives. It reveals God's character in the very beauty, function and existence of every living thing. Yet, it is not only in every living thing. It is in the sunshine, in rainstorms, in the laughter we hear, the health we enjoy, the food we eat, friends and family. It is what meets our needs, answers our prayers, opens the doors of opportunity, employment and closes those same doors (Jeremiah 14:22, Matthew 5:44-45, Acts 14:16-17). It is in His common grace where we see God actively working to control every molecule. A god who did not control every molecule would never be big enough to be worshipped (1 Samuel 2:6, 1 Chronicles 29:11-12, Job 12:23, Job 42:2, Psalms115:3, Isaiah 46:9-10, Ecclesiastes 7:13-14, Isaiah 45:7, Daniel 2:21, Acts 17:24-28). If He did not control every molecule then He could also never offer transforming, saving grace. The Bible is full of God's common grace but it is also full of God's transforming, saving grace which is always given freely to all men. This is grace (favor) that saves man from the wrath of God and His need for justice. We never deserve it or are we worthy of it. It is given so that everyone might be in a relationship with Him and know Him (Nehemiah 9:17, Psalms 78:38, Jonah 4:1-2, 1 Pet. 1:10-

12). God never changes and every good and perfect gift comes from Him (James 1:17).

Before the first man was ever created, God set a plan in existence (Acts 2:23, Ephesians 1:4). A plan to show first His character and glory, and second His love towards His creation, US. This is the purpose of the Bible, tell who God is, how we relate to God, what the blueprint is and about the One who would bring the blueprint to completion. It is a story telling not ours (it involves us), but God's. That is why it is an error when it is said that there is a different God in the Old Testament than there is in the New Testament, or that grace does not exist in the Old Testament part of the Bible. It is through this story that we see man choosing to alienate himself and as a result end up being an enemy of God (Colossians 1:21). We see this in the story of Adam and Eve (Genesis 2:4-3:24) choosing not to listen to God, but instead choosing to become best friends with God's enemy and serve themselves (Ephesians 2:2-3). Yet, it is also the story of how God desired to show His glory, mercy and love but most of all His grace (favor) to those He created to be His excellent ones (Psalms 16:3). It is the story of how He chased them, redeemed them and as a result restored His relationship with them, through His grace (Colossians 1:23).

It is in this story we find God's greatest gift, the gift of His transforming, saving grace first being given to man, through Jesus Christ. It is here where we find the words of Paul in Romans 5:6-11 come alive,

> Christ died for us at a time when we were helpless and sinful. No one is really willing to die for an honest person, though someone might be willing to die for a truly good person. But God showed how much he loved us by having Christ die for us, even though we were sinful. But there is more! Now that God has accepted us because Christ sacrificed his life's blood, we will also be kept safe from God's anger. Even when we were God's enemies, he made peace with us, because

his Son died for us. Yet something even greater than friendship is ours. Now that we are at peace with God, we will be saved by his Son's life. And in addition to everything else, we are happy because God sent our Lord Jesus Christ to make peace with us." Paul would simply express this to Titus as "the grace of God has appeared, bringing salvation for all people (Titus 2:11).

God does not just stop with His transforming, saving grace in bringing us back to a relationship with Him. No, He continues with His transforming grace in what some call His "securing grace." This is the grace that keeps us in this relationship of which He started (Philippians 1:6). We do not just come to Him through grace, but we are kept and move forward in His grace (Galatians 3:2-3). This is why we can know without a shadow of a doubt that through His securing grace we have eternal life (1 John 5:13). Through His sanctifying grace He is making us new (2 Corinthians 5:17), returning us back to not only our original created designed purpose but making us Christlike (1 Peter 2:9-10, 2 Corinthians 5:17). We find His securing and sanctifying grace in the category of His transforming, saving grace. Also through His transforming, saving grace we find His empowering grace. (God not only saves us but He freely gives us the strength to make choices that reflect a heart of gratitude for saving us.)

Empowering grace is the grace that He gives us to live not like we used to or make the same old choices, but to make choices now that represent that we are filled with His Spirit (Ephesians 1:13,14; 4:30). The Holy Spirit points us to truths and reminds us of the truths God has already shown us (John 14:26). As this occurs we are able to produce characteristics and act in ways that represent God (Ephesians 4:25-32). His empowering grace allows us to make choices that produce qualities that represent our identity now that we are in Christ (Galatians 5:16-25). Yet it is not in our strength we are able to do these things but through the Holy Spirit working through the empowering grace of God (Colossians 1:11, 2 Timothy 2:1). This is the beauty of God's transforming, saving grace that is given unmerited to all who place their faith in Christ for eternal life.

In grace both common and transforming, saving we see a quality of God's character that does not exist in man. Because God is pure, His grace must be and that is why grace is 100% God's work. At no time can grace be dependent on how the one who it is given to responds to it, otherwise it would no longer be pure. At a time when we were the first walking dead, when we thought every day should be happy hour and where we desired nothing less than to be left to ourselves, God extended His grace to us to rescue us from Hell. Even when we did not know we needed to be rescued. If we could contribute towards grace or we could do something to merit it we would always want to brag about it and more than likely exaggerate our side of it to make us feel important. Like the fisherman who catches the big fish as he spins his story we would be no different. We would tell others "You ought to see how I helped God with my grace." This is why Paul said in, Ephesians 2:9, "not a result of works, so that no one may boast" (ESV). Having our impure hands (Job 25:4) in it would then make it impure and God is pure, so grace must be.

Grace given freely at God's expense through Christ (Isaiah 53) does not do away with God's other qualities of justice and holiness (Romans 5:10-21). Yet, where the law could not fulfill those qualities or enable us to fulfill those qualities, grace brings to fulfillment those qualities (Galatians 2:21). God's law is what the Bible tells us to do, which goes way beyond the Ten Commandments. God's justice demanded that someone pay the penalty for our failure to live in a way that pleased God or was representative of His character of perfection. This is what we call sin and here is where the story of transforming saving grace begins, through Christ. Christ was the only one who could pay the penalty that God's justice demanded, which He did through the cross. It is through grace that God accepts Christ's obedience to what God requires, as ours (2 Corinthians 5:18-21). This is how grace fulfills the demands of His holiness.

The more we look at grace we discover why it is not only the greatest gift God has given to man but that it is God's overriding quality in how He deals with men in all of life. Whatever happens in our lives comes through this wonderful gift, no matter if it is in His giving or in His denying. Both are precious gifts from God designed for our best. Grace is such a powerful theme that Paul opens and closes each letter with grace and the Bible ends with John wishing God's grace on all who read his letter. Yet the greatest gift to us is the thing we despise, reject and misunderstand the most because the way we are used to thinking and living is completely opposite of the entire concept of grace. Even there we find what grace is, as it expresses that God character of Gods that is not only opposite of man but not found purely in a man. In fact whatever man thinks or does God's ways are not only different but better, beginning with grace (Isaiah 55:9).

Can grace be defined?

Imagine tomorrow you receive news that you are going stone cold deaf. The sounds of life, the wonder of the voices that you hear and the music that invites passion within you will soon be gone. You strive to find an answer, you go beyond the original diagnosis and to doctor after doctor. You see the very best doctors in the world looking for an answer. And yet, time is running out. Soon the wonderful melodic sounds you hear, not just the tiny nuances but the whole ability to hear those you love, will be gone.

You now have seen, so you think, all the doctors who could possibly provide answers and all have said one thing: There is absolutely no hope! So you give up and accept that this is indeed what God has designed for you, a life of utter silence. The pain, the agony of knowing that the day is no longer years away but months away. The sounds of silence become a part of life but not in a treasured way, as in all of us welcome a bit of silence. They become a part of your life in a very painful way, making life at times seem unbearable. Then one day you are told of another doctor who is doing wonderful work. At the insistence of loved ones, you go. After months of testing, a device is surgically installed which enables you to hear and now where once silence reigned supreme, you hear the symphonic sounds of life again! Where once all hope had been lost, new hope has now been given, and as a result, life has been returned to a point where it is no longer deeply painful.

There are many different stories where hope can be lost, from a crippling trauma or life-threatening illnesses, the threat of the loss of a child, even the loss of your home. Often when such events bring the loss of hope, it takes outside intervention to step in and restore, some miraculous event or someone who has an answer that brings hope. Rarely are we able on our own to do something to restore that lost hope. While many may not have personally experienced such events, all of us who live on this round blue marble have been condemned to a different kind of hopelessness.

All of us are just moments away from the train named Eternity running us over as we lie tied to the railroad tracks of condemnation by ropes of our making. (We are condemned to spend eternity away from God because we fall short of God's character of perfection.) These ropes are made by the choices that we make that are contrary to the choices God wants us to make. We willingly make these choices revealing that we are not capable of living how we were designed to live. These choices are what is known as sin or man's continued failure to meet the standards of God, which is perfection.

Our sins that have left us with no hope but to spend an eternity away from the **One** who is deeply passionate about us. Sins that have condemned us and left us destined to an eternity with no hope of life.

Helplessly and hopelessly we lie on those tracks held hostage by our sins until someone tells us, that while the Creator of the universe demands a ransom, one that we are unable to pay, no matter how good a life we live. The ransom God demands is to satisfy his need for justice because we constantly fall short of God's perfection. Yet, because of the Creator's great mercy and passionate love for us, **He** has paid the ransom! We are told in the Bible (which is His Word) that He paid it because of His desire to showcase His greatness, His unconquerable goodness and generosity and His love towards us. The cost of this ransom was the highest ever paid — the life of His Son. The sacrifice that paid the ransom was perfect and needed no additional sacrifices, so there is no cost to us who have been saved and given new hope.

There grace is defined. God's love is the reason He has given us hope, where only eternal separation from God once existed. It is a hope of freedom that comes not from merit but from sacrifice, and not our sacrifice, but Christ's. The hope and freedom is offered to condemned slaves, not because they earned it, but precisely because they could not earn it. We are the condemned slaves who not only have been condemned by the guilt of our failure to meet God's standard, but are tied to the chains of shame from the wrong choices we make. We are also chained and enslaved to serve nothing but ourselves and Satan.

Here in the stanza of an old hymn, we find the simplicity and power of God's love for us.

> O how He loves you and me,
> O how He loves you and me,
> He gave His life, what more could He give?
> O how He loves you, O how He loves me,
> O how He loves you and me.
>
> Jesus to Calv'ry did go,
> His love for mankind to show;
> What He did there bro't hope from despair:
> O how He loves you, O how He loves me,
> O how He loves you and me.
> (Written by Kurt Kaiser, 1976.)

The shorthand for grace is 'mercy, not merit.' Grace is getting what you don't deserve and not getting what you do deserve. Karma is all about getting what you deserve. Christianity teaches that getting what you deserve is death with no hope of resurrection. Grace is the opposite of karma. While everyone desperately needs it, grace is not about us. Grace is fundamentally a word about God: his un-coerced initiative and per-vasive, extravagant demonstrations of care and favor. It is unearned and unconditional, being freely given to all who believe in Jesus Christ, the Son of God.*

---

*   Justin Holcomb, *On The Grace of God*. Crossway. First Edition. 2013.

What does it mean to "be saved"? What does the word "salvation" mean?

The word or term salvation is taken from a Greek word which means "deliverance," "preservation," and "safety." To understand what takes place when we are saved, it is necessary, unfortunately, to use some "churchy" terms or words. Contrary to popular opinion the big words of faith really are important. In certain teachings of our faith, scripture or grace it is hard to fully explain truth without such words.

Words like "Justification," "Sanctification," and "Glorification" are important in order to understand what happens when someone is saved. Yes, we may not like these multi-syllable, unfamiliar words and sometimes they are used to impress us, especially when simpler words exist, but in this case they really are necessary. So let us look at each of these three big words to see not only what they mean, but what part each plays in our salvation.

They are as follows:

1) **Justification** (the Past) – Being saved from the penalty of sin. This occurs when we first accept God's grace, which leads to our being made brand new and without sin. At this point our sins are forgiven, entirely and completely. We are delivered from sin's penalty. One simple choice leads to a single act of God, that results in **His** imparting Christ's righteousness to us.

As a result of Christ's obedience instead of God holding our failed ability to obey the things the Bible tells us we should do, he no longer does. Then through believing Christ when he said, he paid the price to satisfy God for our failure to obey and that there is nothing left to do we are enabled to have a relationship with the Father.

> *Christ died for us at a time when we were helpless and sinful.* [7] *No one is really willing to die for an honest person, though someone might be willing to die for a truly good person.* [8] *But God showed how much he loved us by having Christ die for us, even though we were sinful.*

⁹ But there is more! Now that God has accepted us because Christ sacrificed his life's blood, we will also be kept safe from God's anger.¹⁰ Even when we were God's enemies, he made peace with us, because his Son died for us. Yet something even greater than friendship is ours. Now that we are at peace with God, we will be saved by his Son's life. (Romans 5:6-10)

They replied, "Have faith in the Lord Jesus and you will be saved! This is also true for everyone who lives in your home." (Acts 16:31)

2) **Sanctification** (the Present) – This is the ongoing process where we are being delivered from sin's power. We have been saved from the penalty of our sins and the power of sin in our lives. However it is the working of the Holy Spirit through the grace of God daily that enables us to make choices that do not give sin power over us. It is a work of God, initiated and sustained by Him and is a life-long process through which we, His people, are transformed from God-hating, sin-loving sinners into God-loving, sin-hating saints.

Don't let sin keep ruling your lives. You are ruled by God's kindness and not by the Law. (Romans 6:14)

But I have spoken to you plainly and have tried to remind you of some things. God was so kind to me! (Romans 15:15)

In fact, God thinks of us as a perfume that brings Christ to everyone. For people who are being saved, this perfume has a sweet smell and leads them to a better life. But for people who are lost, it has a bad smell and leads them to a horrible death.

No one really has what it takes to do this work.¹⁷ A lot of people try to get rich from preaching God's message. But we are God's sincere messengers, and by the power of Christ we speak our message with God as our witness. (2 Corinthians 2:15-21)

> *I pray that God, who gives peace, will make you completely holy. And may your spirit, soul, and body be kept healthy and faultless until our Lord Jesus Christ returns.* (1 Thessalonians 5:23)

Here I am being saved daily, hourly, minute by minute from the effects and consequences of sin. In fact, just an hour ago, God's Holy Spirit alerted me to a step which would have led to sin. Public confession or confession with my mouth definitely serves to aid in my becoming more Christ-like. This is described in the passage of Romans 10:9-10:

> *So you will be saved, if you honestly say, "Jesus is Lord," and if you believe with all your heart that God raised him from death.[10] God will accept you and save you, if you truly believe this and tell it to others.*

3) **Glorification** (the Future) — As I am saved from the presence of sin, God promises I will join Him in a glorification, that is, the future perfection which will take place when as a Believer I inherit my home in Heaven, and live eternally in a new God-given body.

[Jesus said,] *"But if you do eat my flesh and drink my blood, you will have eternal life, and I will raise you to life on the last day."* (John 6:54)

> *All of you have faith in the Son of God, and I have written to let you know that you have eternal life.* (1 John 5:13)

There are often many mistakes here as mentioned previously because of the failing to understand these terms. Most of the mistakes fall into one of three areas:

1) Forgetting or not knowing or not bothering to learn that there are indeed three different tenses of the words "saved" and "salvation" as it is referred to in the New Testament. This often

results in the words and terms being confused and used inter-changeably.

2) Failing to remember that salvation is a complete work of God from beginning to end. We have no part in it. God initiates it, empowers it, and enables us to live out His work through the Holy Spirit. We do have a responsibility, though. We are responsible for making choices, empowered by the Holy Spirit, every day in faith and in obedience motivated out of gratitude for the grace God gives new each day. Choices that reflect a heart of gratitude for the precious gift of Salvation God has given all of us.

> *God is the one who began this good work in you, and I am certain that he won't stop before it is complete on the day that Christ Jesus returns* (Philippians 1:6).

Forgetting this important point always leads to some form of legalism in which we attempt to earn, maintain, sustain, keep, or balance out the grace gift of God.

3) Getting justification confused with sanctification. When we keep them separate, we will always have a clearer understanding of God's Word.

If I resist the grace of God can I lose my salvation?

We all resist the grace of God daily in our lives. We think we can live this life on our own or God is interested in the ledger of good deeds and righteous works I am keeping and considers what I can do or not do in order to impress Him.

We are the ones Peter speaks of in 2 Peter 1:5-9.

> *For this very reason, make every effort to supplement your faith with virtue, and virtue with knowledge, ⁶ and knowledge with self-control, and self-control with steadfastness, and steadfastness with godliness, ⁷ and godliness with brotherly affection, and brotherly affection with love. ⁸ For if these qualities are yours and are increasing, they keep you from being ineffective or unfruitful in the knowledge of our Lord Jesus Christ. ⁹ For **whoever lacks these qualities** is so nearsighted that he is blind, having forgotten that he was cleansed from his former sins.* (ESV, my emphasis)

1 John 1:8 gives the unvarnished answer to the question of our spiritual state: "If we say that we have no sin, we deceive ourselves, and the truth is not in us." We **are** the ones who lack Peter's quoted qualities and are failing.

In our own self-sufficiency and self-reliance we are not looking for the grace of God. In our pride and grace-averse hearts, we work to keep logs and account books of the works we do and good deeds we do, believing that we must still do more to impress God, rather than realizing Christ said **"It is finished"** (John 19:30).

Christ was the perfect sacrifice and the only acceptable sacrifice. The single sacrifice that could satisfy God's need for justice (Romans 5:15-17).

We will continually sin, resist God's grace, try to impress God, balance grace, justify ourselves to God and others, remain self-reliant, grace averse and live as we please. That is why grace is a free gift. God is pure, so are His gifts. Grace is one of those gifts and why it is given freely, regardless of how we respond. If it was in response or given and pulled back because we did nothing with it, abused it, did not do what God asked us to do it would not only not be a free gift, it would also not be pure. As a result it would not be from God. Not to mention that it would no longer be grace (Romans 11:6). God did not want us bringing our ledgers and books of good works to Him saying, "Look what I did." It is totally 100% a work of God (Ephesians 2:8-10).

Thanks be to God it is, because we would surely mess it up! Because it is a work of God we know He is faithful to finish what He started (Philippians 1:6). The greatest proof that we have that God will finish what He has started, that we will indeed one day rise again with completely new bodies is the very resurrection of Christ Himself (1 Corinthians 15:12-58).

To make sure we knew it was completely His work and that He would finish it, He gave us His Holy Spirit as a promise or seal (KJV) of our inheritance (Ephesians 1:13-14). In Scripture, a seal signifies:

- A finished transaction (Jeremiah 32: 9-10, John 17:4)
- Ownership (Jeremiah 32:11-12, 2 Timothy 2:19)
- Security (Esther 8:8, Daniel 6:17, Ephesians 4:30)

So yes, you will resist God's grace just like the rest of us, but God knows this. He expected it and made sure your salvation is secured not because of what you do or don't do but because of what **His** Son did. Nor are we responsible for finishing the job as every step of salvation is dependent 100% on His grace. His grace really is sufficient even for our messed up theology, weak attempts to please, half-hearted obedience, divided worship and weak sacrifice.

Still some are bound to bring up how John said that those who "abide in him ought to walk like Christ" (1 John 2:5-6) and John quotes Christ in John 15:4, "Abide in me, and I in you. As the branch cannot bear fruit by itself, unless it abides in the vine, neither can you, unless you abide in me." So what does the word "abide" here mean or what is it referring to?

The word abide here refers to staying connected to Christ or in a relationship with **Him**. What is it that keeps us in that relationship with Christ?

Some would say that it is our obedience, but we have covered that none of us are perfectly obedient. If it is based on our obedience does that mean that when we are just the little bit disobedient God kicks us out. Sort of like, "OK, you did not thank Me over there so because of that you're out of here." Some would say it is not the least sins but when your life does not reflect God's standard of living. The only issue with that is that's our standard; God's standard is perfection. Since none of us are perfect none of us will ever be obedient enough to enable us to stay in a relationship with Christ, within on our own ability.

There is another answer given to what enables us to stay connected to Christ here in this passage. That answer would be our faith. When we place our faith in Christ's finished work God imparts Christ's perfect obedience to us. Thus making it not about our obedience, but **His** obedience to God's laws (The things the Bible tells us to do, which is a lot more than God's moral law). After all, while we will always fail, He never does. Then through our faith the Holy Spirit works to keep us connected to or in a relationship with Christ. We need always remember that our salvation is a total work from beginning to end completed by God. Remembering this is God's work makes faith the accurate answer to the question of what keeps us abiding or connected to Christ.

Then motivated by gratitude for the grace we are given daily we make choices, choices to be obedient to God. As we offer our lives back to Christ. This is the choosing to "abide in him; that, when he shall appear, we may have confidence, and not be ashamed before him at his coming (1 John 1:28).

However, even here the apostle John knows we will not always make the healthy choice that is based on our identity as a disciple of Jesus. John lets us know that the Holy Spirit not only teaches what choices to make but also enables us to make those choices. He is the same one who covers us and keeps us secure when we succeed, do it half-way or just miss it altogether.

> *I am writing to warn you about those people who are misleading you. 27 But Christ has blessed you with the Holy Spirit. Now the Spirit stays in you, and you don't need any teachers. The Spirit is truthful and teaches you everything. So stay one in your heart with Christ, just as the Spirit has taught you to do.* (1 John 2:26-27)

We are either in the process of resisting God's truth or in the process of being shaped and molded by his truth.*

---

*   Charles Stanley, *How To Listen To God.* Thomas Nelson. 2002, p. 19

What happens if I go on sinning?

Count on it! As you do, you will join the rest of us who continue to do so on a daily basis. As John said, "If we say we have no sin, we deceive ourselves, and the truth is not in us" (1 John 1:8).

You may hear other people say, "Be careful of teaching grace in such a way that it encourages others to keep on sinning."

Paul was afraid of encountering this same fear, which is why he wrote Romans 6:1-14. Like Paul, we encourage you now to offer your bodies as instruments of God's glory. It is important to understand that those warning you about this gift of grace have created their own list of little laws, their lists of acceptable or not acceptable sins. The problem with this is that God's standard is the ultimate standard and God's standard is perfection. "But you must always act like your Father in heaven" (Matthew 5:48). None of us, no matter how hard we try, will ever be perfect and we will always sin. This is why salvation must be 100% a complete work of God's to which we can contribute nothing.

When someone who claims to be a disciple of Christ continues to do things that are not glorifying to God, well-intentioned Christians will correct them with a law or instruction on how they should be living or what God's Word says about what they are doing. There is only one issue with this and that is it rarely corrects the long-term, under-lying problem, "for the letter (law) kills but the Spirit gives life" (2 Corinthians 3:6). Our problem which brings us to sin is not always a habit that needs correcting but an identity issue. We need reminding of our true identity, our new identity in Christ and what it cost for us to have that identity. Without a deep understanding of that cost and our lives without Christ no instructions on how to live will ever be lasting.

We see an example of Paul doing this with a church full of "those sanctified in Christ Jesus" who are living in ways that do not glorify God (1 Corinthians). The whole church of Corinth was affected as a result of these individuals. However Paul does not begin the letter of Corinthians dealing with these issues but by first reminding them of the gospel. The gospel is that while we were distanced from God because of our sin, God chased us and brought us near through Christ's sacrifice (Ephesians 2:11). If he pointed out where they were failing without reminding them of who they are, more rebellion could occur. The best way to help our brothers and sisters live in a way that shows a heart of gratitude for God loving us even when we were unlovable is not always giving them a lesson in "How To" first. Sometimes depending on the severity of the sin it is better to start with reminding them who they are first and God's love for them. Then once they are reminded, they will often admit "Yes, I'm not doing what I should be doing." Then a better opportunity comes to talk to them about how to make better choices.

Stop just for a minute and picture what Christ must have seen in the garden which caused Him to be shaken to His very core that His sweat became drops of blood. Then, because it glorified God to exhibit love towards us, Jesus marched forward. Pondering that it was our condition in sin that Christ saw, the wrath of God that was aimed at us, this is what kept Christ on the cross with the need to satisfy God's judgment of sin, which is our failure to live in a way that would please God or reveal God's character. The emptied tomb should be the chief motivation to "doing all things to God's glory" (1 Corinthians 10:31) and living a life of as a vessel reflecting His character.

Focusing on this cannot but help increase our heart of gratitude. As this increases so does our desire to focus more on Christ and say "I love You" through obedience to the Father. In doing this, our view, our sight line, begins to create a type of tunnel vision on the majesty of the Father and the awesomeness of Christ. When this occurs, we see a life that reveals less of the effects of sin and more of the changes brought about through the beauty of grace. That is called living to our identity in Christ.

As you choose to make decisions on who you are now in Christ, through the power of the Holy Spirit, rather than who you were before Christ you will find yourself making choices that reflect that new identity. The more of these choices you make the less you will sin. Though sometimes it will still feel like your making more of the wrong choices than the right ones. God understands, has forgiveness waiting when you repent (change your mind) and opens arms wide to reveal His Love.

May we ask God to surround us instead with friends who may speak the truth and encourage us on how to get it right, but more importantly, they are willing to do an emotional fireman's carry to the One who already got it right, and hold us there until we can imitate Him.

Can I know for sure I have eternal life?

This is a great question, a common one, and yet one that can cause much confusion when answering. The confusion comes from a heart that is really having difficulty grasping the words of Christ when He said "It is finished" (John 19:30). In a world where the sentiment exists that there is no such thing as a free ride, it is indeed hard to grasp that the grace (favor) God gives each of us, to come and accept Christ as our Saviour is freely given, requiring nothing more from us. When every day we must work to achieve, we must meet someone's expectations of us or some of the burdens we often bear. Even if those expectations are to be a good wife, husband, child, or parent. Not to mention the expectations that our employers, customers, teachers, friends or just society in general places on us. Now comes news that there is something that is totally different than everything else that we have been taught, lived by or believed.

That is the beauty of the gospel of grace. It is new news, not old news or old news packaged in a new wrapping. It really is new news, that is contrary to the news our hearts have come to believe. In fact our hearts have been so conditioned by the way this world thinks that they are indeed grace-averse. Robert Capon articulates brilliantly the prayer of the grace-averse heart:

> Lord, please restore to us the comfort of merit and demerit. Show us that there is at least something we can do. Tell us that at the end of the day there will at least be one redeeming card of our very own. Lord, if it is not too much to ask, send us to bed with a few shreds of self-respect upon which we can congratulate ourselves. But whatever you do, do not preach grace. Give us something to do, anything; but spare us the indignity of this indiscriminate acceptance.

That is why the concept of grace being a free gift (Something we do not deserve) is so foreign to us. We desperately want something to hold onto, to claim some ownership of, to know that we met some standard that we could claim some form of redeeming quality about ourselves. We want to know that we could live in such a way that would gain God's pleasure or favor. The truth though is that we cannot. Paul said, in Romans 3:23, "All of us have sinned and fallen short of God's glory." He also said, in Galatians 2:16, "But we know that God accepts only those who have faith in Jesus Christ. No one can please God by simply obeying the Law. So, we put our faith in Christ Jesus, and God accepted us because of our faith."

In other words even if we could perform perfectly the things God has told us to do, it would still not be enough because keeping the laws of God will never enable us to have a right standing before God. Truth is we could never do it perfectly and as a result could never satisfy the need that God has for His justice to be met. God demands justice for our sin. Just as when someone commits a crime they must pay a penalty or carry out a sentence so must we for failing to live in a way that meets God's character of perfection.

Because we cannot do this is why we are condemned to spend eternity separated from Him. What the Bible refers to as Spiritual death. This is the death that Paul speaks of in Romans 6:23, "Sin pays off with death. But God's gift is eternal life given by Jesus Christ our Lord." **Oh!** And what a gift it is!

A gift we can have no part in, for if we could we would make an absolute mess of it. **No!** It is a gift that comes through not earning, not performing, not working to maintain, earn or sustain, after all what kind of gift would that be. It comes through us placing our faith in the finished work of Christ and not our own abilities. Since it comes through the sacrifice of Christ and is a gift is why we can now know for sure that we have eternal life. This is the message of 1 John 5:13 which says, "that you who believe in God's Son will know beyond the shadow of a doubt that you have eternal life" (The Message).

In John 10:28, Christ said "and I give them eternal life, so that they will never be lost. No one can snatch them out of my hand." The "them" here means anyone of us. In other words we can never take ourselves or be taken out of Christ's hands. Now that is security, to know that we can't even work our way out of God's hands. Often, as we walk this life of grace, there will be times we will be like the kid in the grocery store trying to squirm out of our mom or dad's hands. Just like when we were kids, we wanted to run wild and free, untethered to anyone, we wanted to explore, have fun and do as we please. We often will live our lives, serve God, or walk this journey of grace doing just as we please. In fact we will do that more often than we will not. Just as when we tried to squirm out of our mom and dad's hands and they gripped tighter, so does God. The joy robbing pain of everyday living may often cause us to doubt not only our faith but God's love. It is during such times of doubt he grabs hold of our hand tighter as he gently whispers "I love you so much." There really is nothing that can separate us from His radical, passionate love towards us He calls His children (Romans 8:38-39).

Not only is our gift of salvation the greatest gift we will ever receive, it is the only gift we will ever get that never stops giving. We do not just come into a relationship with Christ through grace given freely, it is that same grace God gives new each day that ensures as Paul said in Philippians 1:6, "that He (God) won't stop before it is complete (making us into Christ's image) on the day that Christ Jesus returns (ESV)." We do not just get saved through grace, but we continue in our relationship with Christ through the Holy Spirit as He finishes this work. Making us new; making us into who we were designed to be (Galatians 3:2-5). Even as we choose to live in obedience out of a grateful heart, it is not in our strength that we do so, but because we are strengthened to do so by that very same grace given freely through Christ (2 Timothy 2:1, ESV). There really is nothing we can do, nor do we have any part in making sure that when Christ returns we are presented to God blameless (God will not hold anything against us, 1 Thessalonians 5:23).

In a world demanding us to perform and meet standards to qualify to be accepted. Where everyday it seems just living life is an ever increasing weight of burden. Where it just seems that we will never make it, where some have even stopped trying and the acceptance and approval we seek seems so far out of reach. Where the to do lists seem to get longer and the list of people we need not fail, we need to please grows larger by the day. There is great comfort in knowing that God always finishes His to do list. His number one priority on that list is those He calls His own (Psalms 33:10-11). Because God has promised to finish what He started and because our salvation is 100% His work. We no longer need to meet someone else's standards, list of qualifications or fear the disapproval of others. God has already qualified us. Made us accepted to Him, through Christ and made us ready for the inheritance He has waiting for us (Colossians 1:12-14, ESV).

So we can rest assured, have no doubt that it is not about our ability to be obedient but it is about Christ's ability to do so. We do not retain the gift because we are able to live a life pleasing to God but because Christ did (2 Corinthians 3:4-5, ESV). Because it is about Christ's obedience and not our failure is also why Paul said, "there is no more condemnation (penalty of shame or disapproval from God) for those who are in Christ Jesus" and that "no-one could condemn us" (Romans 8:1, 34). The attacks of others because they feel we are not meeting up to their standards or the shame we used to feel or still feel no longer needs to cause us to feel we will never make it, we just can't do it. Truth is, we cannot, but Christ could. God no longer holds any accusations against us and if He does not no-one else, including ourselves, matters.

Continuing in this walk and in our relationship does not happen by looking to how obedient, deserving, holy, or responsible we are but to the One who brought us into a relationship with Him and will one day finish the work of changing us and making us into His image (Hebrews 12:2). It is because He is working on our behalf and because He became sin for us and continues to intercede (go before the Father on our behalf) for us, that we can now be one hundred percent sure, without a doubt that we have life eternal. Christ was perfect but in order so that we might be able to stand before God blameless, on the cross he took on all the things we have ever done wrong and will do wrong. In other words Christ went "It's on me. I got this," for our sin. He paid the bill for our debt of sin.

I know I belong to Christ because I have believed in Jesus Christ as my only Savior and Redeemer from eternal destruction. It's not the evidences of my life that are my basis for knowing that. It's the Word of God. God said it. That settles it.*

---

* Earl Radmacher, *The Grace Evangelical Society News*. Vol. 10. No.3. May-June 1995.

What about repentance?

The first thing we need to do is to define the word **repentance**. Repentance means to change one's mind. We change our mind about God, His ways, or how we live our life in the light of God's Word. This change of mind usually results in a change of direction, in the way we may be living.

Now here is the tricky part, there is not a time frame, or a time limit, or a duration or an expiration date on either the change of mind or the result of that change of mind. Often we may spend years reflecting or living in a way that seems against God's Word. If we have accepted Christ as our Savior, we should know the Holy Spirit is always at work in our hearts, pointing to truth. Once we accept the truth and realize we need to change our minds regarding that thing which is sinful, it may take time to correct or it may happen overnight for that change of mind to reflect in an outward transformation.

This is why it may seem as though others are not getting the message. As there may be no visible signs that they are indeed changing or making better choices or that they just keep doing the same things over and over. We will do this ourselves, we will know we need to make better choices, act differently, but we will go to God, confess and go right back out and do the same thing all over again. This is why looking to what we should be doing will not be enough by itself to bring change. We need to constantly allow the Holy Spirit over time to bring those changes. As he reminds us of God's love, mercy and other truths. So breathe in deep, take yourself off the hook and rest in knowing God is at work. Be gentle with yourself and others as God through the Holy Spirit brings change.

While it is indeed very important to live for God, to be instruments that truly bring glory to God, to bear fruit in our lives, James said in his letter, "without works your faith is dead" (2:14). My faith is useless. Contrary to what is often taught, James was not saying if you do not have works, you're not saved. What he was saying was if you are claiming to be saved, you may well be.

But your faith is worthless and doing no one else any good if it does not show in your actions.

Now having said that, we never know the heart work that is going on in someone's life. Where they may be in their sanctification process (being made into the image of Christ as we choose to allow sin to have less and less power in our daily lives). This is why God said in 1 Samuel 16:7 "People judge others by what they look like, but I judge people by what is in their hearts." We are all guilty of judging someone's life and then questioning where they are with Christ. It is important to remember that we can never use outward actions or whether we see anyone, including ourselves, becoming more like Christ as a sign of our own or anyone else's salvation or eternal security. We must always rely on the blood of Christ.

> *Then Christ went once for all into the most holy place and freed us from sin forever. He did this by offering his own blood instead of the blood of goats and bulls.* (Hebrews 9:12)

> *My friends, the blood of Jesus gives us courage to enter the most holy place[.]* (Hebrews 10:19)

Often many are placed on the hooks of guilt as they wonder whether they have repented **enough** or if they have repented for everything. Yet here is the reality: Our sins are so numerous that we could never confess them all or repent for all of them! The psalmist said, "For evils have encompassed me beyond number; my iniquities have overtaken me, and I cannot see; they are more than the hairs of my head; my heart fails me" (Psalm 40:12, ESV).

So we can be thankful that "**He** does not deal with us according to our sins" (Psalm 103:10, ESV), but according to **His** grace. Grace that has been given to all and "There is therefore now no condemnation for those who are in Christ Jesus" (Romans 8:1, ESV). So yes, by all means let us seek to confess those sins the Holy Spirit brings to mind. He identifies our sins, not with shame, but with His grace, which is exhibited through loving open arms to remind us of how much He loves us. And we learn to accept the forgiveness that He has awaiting for us, also through His grace (already paid for, freely given through the perfect sacrifice of Christ). May we live in such a constant remembrance that God has covered those things we do wrong (sins) and, as such, ask for the strength to accept the forgiveness that awaits us, so that the guilt of such sin does not render us ineffective as His chosen vessel. (We have not only been chosen by God to be his instruments and messengers of grace, love and mercy, but to also reflect His character.)

Another teaching that can run into errors is the belief that we must experience deep sorrow or regret towards those sins. Like a lot of things, there are truths and untruths here. Yes, we should have sorrow when we break God's heart or spit in Christ's face with the way we live. But it is an error when someone else judges the way we live our lives and decides we did not change **enough**. This is why outward actions of change very often do not reflect our new identity and is never an adequate mark.

There is also great confidence and assurance in knowing God does not establish a litmus test as to whether we have confessed enough, shown enough sorrow, and made all the correct actions to show our repentance. The desire to serve God or do things to please Him and the sorrow when we fail to change and live in His way can be a very significant **personal** indicator. That very desire and sorrow we feel may tell us the Holy Spirit is alive and at work in our lives. For without the Holy Spirit's work of pointing us to His truth, we may have no desire to serve anything but ourselves and Satan (Ephesians 2:1-3) as we live "alienated and hostile" (Colossians 1:21), an enemy of God.

> *Even when we were God's enemies, he made peace with us, because his Son died for us. Yet something even greater than friendship is ours. Now that we are at peace with God, we will be saved by his Son's life.* (Romans 5:10)

Another error that often occurs when someone is teaching on repentance and is commonly taught on Sunday mornings is the error that looking at what we have done or not done will always lead to a repentance that leads to a Godly sorrow which results in change. Simply looking at what we are not doing or should be doing and then changing may or may not be nothing more than being a very moral person.

It may or may not reveal a heart filled with gratitude for what Christ did. The "sorrow that leads to repentance" (2 Corinthians 7:10, ESV) that Paul speaks of happens when we look at our failings in the light of God's mercy and grace that was given through the sacrificed Lamb, Jesus Christ. This sorrow helps us focus on what we have done or not done in the light of what perfect obedience looks like through the example of the only one who lived it, Jesus. As that light of the Spirit's truth shines bright, it illuminates for us the change that needs to occur in order for us to focus more on serving others and intimately worship the One who calls us **His** Beloved.

So while repentance in our hearts and minds should always be ongoing and produce the fruit as evidenced by our repentance, we need to be careful not to place our assurance of our relationship with God on anything other than the blood of Jesus Christ.

> Evangelical repentance is repentance of sin as sin: not of this sin nor of that, but of the whole mass. We repent of the sin of our nature as well as the sin of our practice. We bemoan sin within us and without us. We repent of sin itself as being an insult to God. Anything short of this is a mere surface repentance, and not a repentance which reaches to the bottom of the mischief. Repentance of the evil act, and not of the evil heart, is like men pumping water out of a leaky vessel, but forgetting to stop the leak. Some would dam up the stream, but leave the fountain still flowing; they would remove the eruption from the skin, but leave the disease in the flesh.*

---

*   Charles H. Spurgeon, *Metropolitan Tabernacle Pulpit*. Edinburgh: Banner. 1970. Volume 35, 127

Why do I keep sinning?

To be honest all of us have at least one annoying little sin that we just can't keep from repeating, for most it may be something like over eating. Eating is fun, it's enjoyable, it lifts our spirits. Like most things though, if not done in balance, or with care, it can be abused; misused, and just flat out done in a way that can harm us. Overeating is a sin and it is called gluttony. Yet, perhaps that is not yours maybe it is another one that keeps tripping you up. Maybe there is more than one. John really was right when he said in 1 John 1:8, "If we say that we have not sinned, we are fooling ourselves, and the truth isn't in our hearts." We sin because even if only for a minute it's downright fun and pleasurable (Hebrews 11:25). Though ultimately that displeasure only lasts for a minute and then we feel guilty, shame and a whole host of other emotions. This is true of all of us and the main reason is that even though we are saved it does not mean that we do not still struggle with those things that once appealed to us. That we once worshipped, instead of God. In Romans 7:18 Paul said, "I know that my selfish desires won't let me do anything that is good. Even when I want to do right, I cannot."

Coming to Christ does not mean that those things that once grabbed our attention do not any more. It only means that when we choose to worship something other than God or place something smaller than God in a place that only He can or should occupy (And We Will, Count On It!), that it no longer condemns us (separates us from God). For we have been delivered from such condemnation (Romans 8:1, 34). That does not mean that we will not suffer consequences, or the effects of that sin, or that we do not need to change our mind about what we are doing, or confess that sin to God. What it does mean is that before we would not have even recognized, much less cared that it was an offense to God (Ephesians 2:1-3, 4:17-19). Anything short of God's character or perfection is an offense. Now we can recognize it as such and change our mind about what we are doing that is an offense to God. Before we were powerless to do anything about it, now we can. We can confess it to God and accept the forgiveness He eagerly waits to lavish us with (1 John 1:9). Someone though, is bound to tell you that God has not forgiven the sins we will commit in the future. That begs the question: "How many of your sins were in the future when Christ died on the cross?" (Hint: **ALL!**) Rest assured that God awaits with loving open arms to give the forgiveness that has already been paid for.

Johann Arndt in his book *True Christianity* said, it best: "Heart-suffering because of sin is the best proof that the Holy Spirit dwells in your heart."

We have always known the difference between wrong and right, this is the purpose of God's laws. God's laws are what the Bible tells us to do, which goes way beyond the ten commandments. The problem is it is in our nature to rebel, telling us not to do something is the sure fire way to guarantee that we will usually do it. Like telling a two year old, don't do that. We all know how this usually works out. Till we experience something that brings us greater joy than rebelling brings us.

God did not give us laws to get us to stop sinning, but to show us that we could not and as such they would point us to Him for an answer. That answer is called grace. Grace is defined as the saving power of God from sin. Whether that be His favor given to us who do not deserve it and thus saving us from having to pay the penalty of our sin. It can also be God daily through His strength helping us make choices that reflect His character, rather than the choices we used to make. That does not make the law bad for it is as good and is as much needed as grace is. It is never bad law, good grace. The law not only points us to God, but shows us what God's character looks like and how we ought to live. It just can't enable us to live it or restore our relationship with God or deliver us from the shame that comes from our failure to live in a way to please God. In fact, by itself the law will always bring more shame. That is why God gave us grace through Christ Jesus. The mistake is made though when we live as though we must do those things the Bible tells us to do in order to maintain our relationship with God. In other words, we live a law motivated lifestyle. Consequently, we judge the way we live and how others live by the law of God, rather than through God's mercy and love. This is often referred to as legalism.

When we do this we place ourselves in a situation of impossibility (we cannot live in such a way as to please God or earn God's approval) which always results in feelings of deep shame and feelings of failure (Hebrews 11:6). No matter how hard we focus on being more obedient (doing those things the Bible tells us to do), and no matter how hard we focus on not sinning, it will not keep us from sinning. Sin receives its power from the law (1 Corinthians 15:56), in other words it is through the law that we are made to feel guilty, ashamed and it reminds us of how far we fall short of God's character. Without the law there would be no sin (Romans 3:20). So the more we focus on trying not to sin by the sweat of our brow, by working hard to please God, or work to get God's approval the more we will sin. In fact such efforts will have just the opposite effect as not only will it probably have the result of making us demanding and mean to ourselves, but those demands and that meanness will definitely pour out of us into others. This always kills not only our joy of salvation but the joy of others. This is what Paul meant when he said in 2 Corinthians 3:6 "the Law brings death, but the Spirit brings life." So what's the answer? The answer is to stop trying not to sin! Now that seems strange does it not? "Surely we should not sin," you say.

Tomorrow, no matter how hard a dog tries to be a cat he will never be a cat. It is also true that no matter how hard we try to stop sinning we can not. For we are not sinners because we sin, we are sinners who sin (Psalm 51:5, Romans 5:12). That is who we are, we choose to not obey God's laws because it is our nature to do so. We cannot change our nature, but God through His grace can (Romans 6:14, ESV). As His grace begins to change us it will enable us to be able to choose every day to not allow sin to control us or to give it the power over us it once had (Galatians 5:16-25, Ephesians 4:25-32). As we realize that where sin once had complete power over us it no longer does and we have a choice now to serve it or not to. We do not find within ourselves the power (2 Timothy 2:1) to make these choices or does living with a focus on making these choices or not making these choices teach us to do so. For the law can only show what such choices are, it cannot teach us to make those choices, only grace can do that (Titus 2:11-14).

So it is not a focus on our not sinning that allows us to stop sinning but a focus on that while we were without hope we were still passionately loved by God (Romans 5:6-7). Which He exhibits through His grace. It is important as we walk on this journey that we remind ourselves of this truth moment by moment. That does not mean God hates sin any less or takes our sin any lighter (Romans 1:18). God deplores sin and takes sin so seriously that He condemned us to Hell for it (Romans 6:23). What it does mean is that God no longer deals with us, because of Christ, according to our sin (Micah 7:18, Acts 17:11). Now, he deals with us by His grace and the blood of Jesus who has made us clean (without sin!) before God (1 John 1:7).

When we accepted Christ as our savior God placed a new heart and a new spirit within us. In other words he gave us new abilities to make different choices. Choices that reveal that we are now Children of God. Yet, these are brand new abilities given through grace upon our salvation, enabled to be used by the Holy Spirit. God did not take our old abilities, fix them up, put new coats of paint on them, and then enable us to use them in a different way. No these are brand new God given abilities that are only in use when we use them for Him. He also did not give us these new abilities just so that others can see how far we have come or how much we have changed. For indeed, it is not about us, even when we and others want to tell us it is. He has not chased us and brought us near in order that we might one day shout out to the world "I'm Not Who I used To Be." That does not mean He is not changing us, making us new, reshaping us. It only means that it is for His glory and not ours that He is changing us (Ezekiel 36:24-32, 38, Ephesians 2:4). God takes great delight when our focus is not on what we are doing but on who **He** is. The Psalmist said in, Psalm 147:11, "The Lord takes pleasure in those who fear *(Respect)* Him, in those who hope in His steadfast love."

Heavy (spending hours, days, and months thinking about nothing but how bad we have messed up or how bad of a sinner we are) introspection on our sin or about our sin usually comes from an unhealthy spiritual perspective. This can even lead to physical health issues. Reason it is unhealthy is because it will usually be from a point of feeling that we are not meeting up, we are failing, God is displeased with us, others will think bad of us, all of these and any other reason that makes us focus on our sin, is sin. We cannot meet up, the sooner we stop trying to, the sooner we will stop kicking ourselves and switch our focus to the one who begun our faith and will ensure that one day we are a finished product, ready for heaven (Hebrews 12:2). For it is impossible for those who are in God's saving grace, who have been chosen, who are the bride of Christ to not abuse, be ungrateful for or irresponsible with God's grace. The law says there would only be two ways this could happen. The first one being we must be perfect and the second being we do not know Christ as our personal savior.

Accepting that sin no longer has power over us also allows us to no longer feel the need to rebel against the things God asks us to do. As a result, what was once painful and we were unable to choose to do so, becomes our delight (Psalms 112:1). Where we once turned to sin to relieve and bring pleasure even if just for a moment from the pains of everyday living, we will no longer need to. Instead we will find great joy and delight in being passionate about worshipping God and looking to His law in how to be obedient in order to say thank you for loving us first (Romans 7:22).

I am fearful of those today, who because of a genuine, valid concern about the lack of growth and the lack of evident Christian lifestyle, are willing to try to pop up the Gospel by adding to it.[*]

Do I need to make Christ Lord of my life?

Often one will hear the phrase, "Make Jesus the Lord and Savior of your life." What happens if we look at the opposite of that statement, what do we get? "Christ really isn't the Lord of my life." And now some of the consequence questions come to mind:

Does this mean if **I** do not acknowledge Him as Lord, then He is not Lord?

- *David didn't go up to heaven. So he wasn't talking about himself when he said, "The Lord told my Lord to sit at his right side,[35] until he made my Lord's enemies into a footstool for him."[36] Everyone in Israel should then know for certain that God has made Jesus both Lord and Christ, even though you put him to death on a cross.* (Acts 2:34-36)

If Christ is God, then is there still a question that He is Lord?

- *Only I am the Lord!*
  There are no other gods.
  I have made you strong,
  though you don't know me.
  [6] Now everyone from east to west will learn
  that I am the Lord.
  No other gods are real. (Isaiah 45:5-6)

What happens if I don't make Jesus Lord of my life, can I derail God's plans?

- *From the very beginning, I told what would happen long before it took place.*
  I kept my word[11] and brought someone from a distant land to do what I wanted.
  He attacked from the east, like a hawk swooping down.
  Now I will keep my promise and do what I planned.
  (Isaiah 46:10-11)

Does this mean He is not sovereign (supreme ruler) in my life?

- *This God made the world and everything in it. He is Lord of heaven and earth, and he doesn't live in temples built by human hands.²⁵ He doesn't need help from anyone. He gives life, breath, and everything else to all people. 26 From one person God made all nations who live on earth, and he decided when and where every nation would be.*

  ²⁷God has done all this, so that we will look for him and reach out and find him. He isn't far from any of us, 28 and he gives us the power to live, to move, and to be who we are. "We are his children," just as some of your poets have said. (Acts 17:24-28)

Will I hinder Jesus' work in my life?

- Not only do we see in Isaiah 46 that He shall bring His purpose and plans to pass, but we also see in Philippians 1:6 that when God begins a work, He finishes it.

Can I make Christ anything that He is not already?

- Really?! Christ is already Lord of our lives whether we make Him so or not. To make Christ Lord of our lives is often said to make sure we will not go on sinning or live as we please.

But we already looked at the issue that Christ is Lord, whether we make Him so or not and there really is no condemnation to those who are in Christ Jesus. So while we should always live in a way that honors God, be prepared to realize we do not always measure up. That feeling of not measuring up to what God wants us to be is the surest sign that Christ is indeed Lord of our life. Before we accepted the free gift of God, we could not desire anything towards God. Now that we do feel bad when we sin, it is a sign that the Holy Spirit is convicting us of our sins.

And remember, teaching or working hard to make sure we are making Christ Lord of our life is a form of legalism. It is placing ourselves under the law and trying to create a relationship that we think will please God through our own actions. It is the righteousness of Christ that God sees (2 Corinthians 5:21 ESV). What Paul is saying when he says this is that instead of our deeply flawed and often failing obedience to God's perfect law, God now sees the perfect obedience of Christ to His laws. Christ has been and will always be the only one who is able to meet God's standard of perfection.

There is one more point with this thinking. We really will continue to sin no matter what we do. That is why 1 John 1:8 says if we say we are without sin, we lie. Proverbs 4:23 says "Above all else, guard your heart, for everything you do flows from it." It should be said that not only what we do but what we say as well. So the words of our mouth not only reflect our thoughts, but what we often believe. So if we say that we are without sin then that statement may or may not originate from a genuine heart belief. A belief that we are indeed without sin and as a result, not only what we just said, but our thoughts and our very heart may indeed be guilty of lying. Worst of all, we may be lying to ourselves.

We will never be without sin as the definition of sin is not messing up a little. Nor is it not meeting standards set by someone who we trust or value or hold a high opinion of. The definition of sin is falling short of God's standard, His character.

God's standard is perfection and Jesus spoke often that it was more than about being "just good" (Matthew 5:40-48). This is why it is important to realize that while He is always Lord of our lives, the issue is whether or not I am living in a way that represents my new identity as Jesus' disciple, His ambassador to the world. We can be thankful that it is we that change and never Him when we do blow it (and we will!). We can step back, confess our failings, and remind ourselves of who we are and that He is indeed **LORD**!

Do I need to do good works?

Paul said in Ephesians 2:10, "For we are his workmanship, created in Christ Jesus for good works, which God prepared beforehand, that we should walk in them." (ESV) Then he told Titus in 3:8, "These things are excellent and profitable for people."(ESV) So the question is not should we do them, but what is the result if we do not do them?

There is no document that exists that will help us determine if we are doing enough good works. In other words there is nothing that says "Do these things so many times and you will have done enough good works to have God be pleased with you." Yet, often when we look at our own lives, not to mention the lives of others we act as though such a document does exist. We will often treat not only ourselves, but others based on whether we think they are following this imaginary documents guidelines successfully. If we or someone else are not, then we question not only ours, but their relationship with God. If we or they are following this documents, guidelines then we determine that they are indeed living as they should.

While God's Word gives many instructions on what those good works should be and what they will look like, it never gives a quantification of "Well if you're doing 'X amount' of good works, you can truly say that you are doing enough." Though many seem to teach this, Christ had something very powerful to say about this in Matthew 5:20 when He told those who thought they were doing enough — they needed to do more.

Here are some errors to avoid when teaching on the subject of works:

- Judging ourselves or others' personal relationship to God, including His approval or disapproval with us based on the amount of our works. The real truth is, our relationship with the Father should never be based on what we do or do not do, but always on the blood of Christ (Hebrews 10:19).

- Believing that God is keeping a ledger or a book of the good works we do and will one day declare us either righteous or unrighteous based on this accounting. Romans 4:5 says, "But you cannot make God accept you because of something you do. God accepts sinners only because they have faith in him."
- Thinking that God needs our good works and without them we cannot obtain God's grace (love). God needs nothing from us and as a result He does not need our good works. Acts 17:24-25 states "And he is not served by human hands, as if he needed anything. Rather, he himself gives everyone life and breath and everything else." (NIV) Our good works are not for God, they are for the service of others.
- Not realizing it is not us doing the good works but Christ working through us. (Philippians 2:13).
- Failing to understand the very desire to live in a way to honor God is indeed a sign that we are Christ's own. For before we accepted Christ as our Savior, we could not, nor would we desire to, do works pleasing to God (Ephesians 2:1-3).

It is not about your performance or lack thereof, but it is about the ultimate performance which Christ gave. Nor is it about your ability to live in a way that pleases God, good deeds, good works or anything else you might do.

Though we do not base our relationship with God on what we do, the gift of grace God is given to each of us freely, unmerited through the blood of Christ when we did not do anything, could not do anything, did not even know we needed it. We show ingratitude for this precious gift by not making choices every day that reflect the gift God has given us (Ephesians 5:2). When we make these choices we represent a god who does not exist. This is a little god made up of things that we put in places to find comfort, security, power, pleasure and approval in, always smaller than God, Himself. The God who would give such a gift did so because of His great mercy. As it stood in the way of His wrath, in order that we might be brought back into a relationship with Him (Ephesians 2:11). When we do this it hinders not only how we reflect God (Colossians 3:12-14, ESV), but our witness to His glory (1 Peter 2:12). When we do this it will indeed be difficult for others to see that we have chosen Christ as our Saviour (Proverbs 27:19). The greatest reflection that God is at work in us and the Holy Spirit now resides in us is when our life reflects that we find great delight in God's laws (Psalms 112:1). Our mission and passion is found in making Christ known and expressing God's love and grace to others While we can say with words all day that we believe this for others not having the actions (works) to back us up is the very definition of being hypocritical. While we all are! Let us pray that the choices we make reflect how much we understand God loves us, so that others see a life motivated by gratitude. Instead of a life driven by the same things that once motivated us. Living life this way will allow others to see the difference Christ has made in our lives. As a result, they may just want to know more about what has brought the changes in our life. Which will always introduce others to the God who loves them passionately and the one who died so they could live again.

> If you have really handed yourself over to Him, it must follow that you are trying to obey Him. But trying in a new way, a less worried way. Not doing these things in order to be saved, but because He has begun to save you already. Not hoping to get to Heaven as a reward for your actions, but inevitably wanting to act in a certain way because a first faint gleam of Heaven is already inside you.[*]

---

[*]   C. S. Lewis, *Mere Christianity*. Simon & Schuster, 1996, pp. 130-131.

What is the purpose of God's laws now that I am a Christian?

Since we are discussing grace it should be considered with this question. So perhaps the question would become "What role does the **law** play as compared to the role **grace** plays in my life, now that I am a Christian?"

Before we get much further let's place some basic understandings on what the law is and what grace is. So that when we speak of either we have a basic understanding of what we are referring to. God's law are those things in scripture that show us His character, tell us how we were designed to live and what being Christlike (how Christ lived) looks like. Grace is given to us freely and is the lens upon which God views us now. As He views us not through our failure to live in a way that pleases Him but through the perfect obedience of Christ to His law.

A common misconception is that it is either what we must be doing or should do (law) or the unmerited favor of God (grace), not both. In other words, it is all about God's grace. Those who hold to the first will always be pushing the law of God, and as a result will often fall into a legalistic lifestyle or use God's word to threaten others into such a lifestyle. The other half says it is all about God's grace and neglect teaching the law. This will often result in a live-free, do as you please lifestyle. Both of these lifestyles are wrong.

Another error is when God's law and grace are taught in such a way that it combines them and mixes them together. When this occurs the standard of God's law has been lowered to something achievable and that we can live. This teaching is often referred to as moral-ism. So instead of a law that demands absolute perfection, which is what God's law always demands, as it represents God's character, which is perfect. When this occurs we end up with a law that tells us not about God or his character, but how to live with our fellow man and other helpful hints on how to live a happy life. When this happens, grace becomes a tool to threaten us when we fail to do that. As an example, one might hear in such a situation, "How can you be so irresponsible with God's grace?" One hearing that might just simply reply, "Cannot help it, that's why I need God's grace because I am always disobeying His perfect law, and here's a hint, so are you." God's law always reveals God's character of perfection, while His grace is always non-bullying.

Softening God's perfect law or separating it from God's enabling, non-crushing, freeing, non-threatening grace always results in an imbalance and leads to a life lived contrary to what God designed. When we mix the two we always end up softening God's perfect law or weakening God's amazing grace.

Grace is not about a magical number line, numbering from one to ten, and on the number line from 1-5 is grace and then the rest of the way it is grace, plus. Plus, whatever else someone might add to balance, sustain, maintain, make sure grace is not abused, handled irresponsibly or any other condition someone might attach to grace. If there were such a magical number line it would be numbered 1-10 with each number having a giant "G" attached to it. Where the "G" stood for grace, plus nothing.

Grace is not only the seed but the Miracle-Gro® for our walk in grace. It is the very thing that enables us to live the law of God.

Often someone will say that "you cannot teach grace without repentance as it may lead to abuses, misuse of grace and lazy Christianity." Some are quick to point out that "we need to be responsible with grace." While it is true, grace should not be taught without the law and vice-versa. The reasons are never any of the above mentioned reasons. For in truth, the following is true and should always be kept in mind.

1) We cannot balance grace!

2) We can never make ourselves deserving of grace!

3) We cannot maintain, sustain, or keep grace or our relationship with the Father. It really is 100% His work.

4) We always abuse God's grace, all of us!

5) We will always misuse grace, none of us are pure here.

6) We are all lazy Christians, even the most seemingly fervent and righteous of us.

7) The person that is probably most irresponsible with grace stares at us as we brush our teeth.

It is not that the law and grace are in opposition to each other but rather that they have different purposes. For the law cannot make us good enough to please God or righteous, present us finished before God, or bring us to the point in which God is happy with us. That is the work of the Holy Spirit through grace. In fact, if all we did every day was live according to the law with no grace, not only would we slowly die but we would kill those around us maybe even quicker (2 Corinthians 3:6).

What Paul is saying here really does play out in real life. This is the person who is always looking at what they are doing right and wrong and judging themselves. They declare themselves not meeting up to the standards they feel they should live by, according to what they think is God's law. As a result, they become harsher and more demanding on themselves. As they analyze which rules, things they believe the Bible is telling them they should do. (Hint: We All Do This!) The more we feel we are failing the harder we work. We place stricter standards for ourselves to keep others from seeing we are failing. We really want to be seen as having it together and that we are good obedient children, rather than the failures we actually are. This is in essence pride and why James said in, James 4:6, "God opposes the proud, and gives more grace to the humble." It is not that He gives more grace, He's given us all we need. We are just able to apply more of it in our lives. When we stop trying to act as like we are able to do what is pleasing to God through a strict focus on God's laws, we are able to use more of God's strength (grace). After all only Christ could do the things God requires perfectly. Pretending that we can do it and that we are not failing is pride. Yet, when we stop pretending, God enables us to use more of His grace to do the things He asks us to do (2 Timothy 2:1-4) and make choices that reflect His glory, grace and love (Colossians

1:1-4). When we continue to try to do this by looking to those things God asks us to do (God's law) we not only place unrealistic demands on ourselves, but view and treat others through the same lens. So we become demanding and condemning as we look into the lives of others. Rather than treating them with the same love and mercy God gives us. (Hint: We Are All Guilty Of This, Too.) This is living by the law and requiring others to as well, which always has the effect of bringing emotional, spiritual and sometimes even physical death for us and others. Learning to live in grace comes as we moment by moment reflect that we were once God's enemies and there was nothing at all we could do to make ourselves righteous. We could not live in a way that would enable us to meet God's standards or live in a way pleasing to God. But, God still was passionately in love with us. So He chased us and through Christ, He brought us back into a relationship with Him. The more we reflect on this the greater desire it creates within us to reflect how much we are loved by God. It also creates within us a desire to treat others with God's grace rather than expecting them to be something they cannot be, Perfect. This always exhibits God's love. Loving others this way will always have greater impact than any law enforced living ever will. It also helps brings others to get to know who God really is and how much He loves them, which always brings life.

In Romans 4:9-15, Paul tells us that Abraham was not counted righteous because he was circumcised, but was righteous before his circumcision. Because we see that the law brings about wrath, but faith has brought about righteousness. Then in Galatians 2:21 Paul tells us "that if the law could bring about righteousness then Christ died in vain."

The law is a constant reminder of how far short we fall from God's character, His perfection. Because we do, we are deserving of God's wrath. However, we are not counted right with God because we are able to keep the law. Even Abraham was counted right before God because he believed that Christ was coming. If we could do something on our own to make ourselves right before God, then Christ died for nothing.

While the law perfectly tells us we miss the mark of God's perfection which allows it to serve as a reminder of our failure, it also tells us where we need to change and shows us what the change looks like. It is grace which enables that change. With God's grace, we are able to live according to what the law commands. Second Corinthians 9:8 says "that God gives us grace so that we might be able to do every good work."

So if one asks, "Are we under the law?" The answer is **"Yes!"** For the law was never meant to bring life, or be a way that we could make God happy with us. God knows we are human (Psalms 103:14) and as a result will always fail. We are under law because it still serves its original purpose to point us to our need for **grace**, which we need new every day (Lamentations 3:22-23) in order to live a righteous life.

> Picture a parent leading a child to a school bus. The parent explains and shows the child what the right way looks like and instills inside the child what the wrong way is as he takes him to the school bus. The parent is the law and grace is the school bus and you are the child.*

---

* Pastor David Lyles, Connection Fellowship Church, Powdersville, S.C.

I have not been living right and have messed up really bad. Can God still, or will God still, forgive me?

None of us are living right! All of us must go to God moment by moment and confess our sins.

> *If we say that we have not sinned, we are fooling ourselves, and the truth isn't in our hearts. 9 But if we confess our sins to God, he can always be trusted to forgive us and take our sins away.* (1 John 1:8-9)

> *If you keep growing in this way, it will show that what you know about our Lord Jesus Christ has made your lives useful and meaningful.* (2 Peter 1:8)

So yes, God has already forgiven us and is waiting for us to accept His forgiveness.

God is not waiting for us to **do** something for this gift. His forgiveness is not offered as a result of penances, deep holy back-sweating, or sack cloth and ashes rituals.

It is simply offered through a change of mind that comes from a change of heart about the very sin we need to confess to God. We can accept the forgiveness God has already given through the cross.

When Christ died on the cross, everything we have done or will ever do was forgiven. Some may teach that we must confess with a really sorrowful heart our sins and when God hears our sorrow, **He** will forgive.

We can never be sorrowful enough about our sins. Our sins cost Christ His very life. To think that we can now express enough sorrow for our sinful condition shows little understanding of the cost of our forgiveness. Not to mention, it may be nothing more than our inability to realize that we are indeed accepted by God. As we feel if we muster enough sorrow that God will indeed approve us. Nor can we even begin to repent (change our minds about the things we are doing wrong) of all of our sins. This does not mean we should not repent or show sorrow, only that we can never do either sufficiently enough to say we have.

There is another issue with making a statement like this if we say God cannot do something unless **we** first do something, we limit God. We make God's plans and purposes conditional as He stands back saying "Wait, Wait, Wait for it." This could halt His plans and is contrary to Scripture, for we see that God is neither dependent on anyone and does not need something from us. This may or may not be nothing more than a shallow form of repentance. It is not about the single sins we commit but having a heart that reveals that we realize we fall way short of anything pleasing to God, except through Christ.

> *This God made the world and everything in it. He is Lord of heaven and earth, and he doesn't live in temples built by human hands.²⁵ He doesn't need help from anyone. He gives life, breath, and everything else to all people.* (Acts 17:24-25)

No one can halt or stop God's plans and purpose.

> *Now keep this in mind, you sinful people. And don't ever forget it.*

> *I alone am God! There are no other gods; no one is like me. Think about what happened many years ago. ¹⁰ From the very beginning, I told what would happen long before it took place.*

> *I kept my word¹¹ and brought someone from a distant land to do what I wanted. He attacked from the east, like a hawk swooping down. Now I will keep my promise and do what I planned.* (Isaiah 46:8-11)

This is the reason why we know that forgiveness has not only been given in advance but has already been paid for. If forgiveness was based on whether we did it correctly, did it often enough, said all the right words, felt all the right emotions, or anything else we would surely place God in a place that He could not be

God. For His ability to complete His plan that was placed in place before the foundation of the world, would be hindered. As He waited for us to make a move and He could then make a counter move. Instead we can rest in peace knowing His moves are made not in reaction to ours but because it pleases Him. It pleases Him to have us come to His open arms of forgiveness as he showers us not with guilt and shame but His amazing love.

We must always remember God does what He does because it pleases **Him** to glorify Himself not because of us (Psalms 135:6). Even the good deeds we do, it is **Him** working through us to do those things (Philippians 2:13). The apostle Paul says, "I have been crucified with Christ. It is no longer I who live, but Christ who lives in me. And the life I now live in the flesh I live by faith in the Son of God, who loved me and gave himself for me" (Galatians 2:20, ESV). This is a forgiveness that has already been given, is waiting for us and all we have to do is accept it. Remember God does not deal with us according to our sin, for He remembers that we are but human (Psalms 103:10-14).

Often we might have trouble accepting God's forgiveness and want to keep kicking and beating ourselves up. Rest assured condemnation is not from God, for "there is no condemnation to those who are in Christ Jesus" (Romans 8:1). And no one else can condemn you either (Romans 8:34).

So confess those things you have done wrong not to get but to receive God's forgiving love. Do not let yourself or anyone else keep you from believing that God is still not dealing with you according to His grace.

It's in the past, God's forgiven it, so I can move on without talking or dealing with anyone else, right?

The answer to that question depends. If what we have done wrong is a personal issue, then it is between God and us. Once we have confessed and accepted God's forgiveness then it is indeed in the past.

Now, habitual sin is another issue. Habitual sins are ones we keep doing and will continue to do, unless we get help. We should seek counsel for and wisdom in how to overcome and deal with them. This does not mean that God has not forgiven them, it just means in order for us to keep these things from hindering us from living according to the purpose upon which we were created, we need help. Proverbs, an excellent book of wisdom, tells us that "iron sharpens iron" (Proverbs 27:17). Getting proper help will help us live to glorify God.

If your sin is something which has occurred between you and another person, Scripture is clear on this as well. We must be willing to forgive. Just as Christ has forgiven us, so we are to forgive as well.

> *Put up with each other, and forgive anyone who does you wrong, just as Christ has forgiven you.* (Colossians 3:13)

If we are the one at fault, we must go quickly to that person and deal with it (Matthew 5:24). This should be done before any other service to others or gifts given to God takes place. Once we have confessed to God and gone to the one we have injured and asked for forgiveness, we have done our responsibility. From there it is their responsibility to forgive — or not.

The opposite is also true. If we are the one who has been injured, we need to first forgive the person in our heart. Then we should be willing to go to that brother or sister and speak about how they have offended us. If they come to us first, we should be willing and open to a conversation and allow them to share completely what they may have done wrong. Confession really does bring healing, and without it, healing rarely occurs.

> *Therefore, confess your sins to one another and pray for one another, hat you may be healed. The prayer of a righteous person has great power as it is working.* (James 5:16)

The importance of open and honest relationships with our brothers and sisters in Christ cannot be overstated. We are not meant to be individual Christians living this life apart from each other. We are meant to be in community. It is the ongoing interactions, time we spend with each other, that truly does play a pivotal role in our sanctification (being able to make choices and live like Christ), as God works through each other to sharpen each other (Hebrews 3:13, Hebrews 10:24-25).

We also find that the more we grow in our understanding of our own need for the ugliness of the cross, the less we will be concerned with the faults of others. This will allow us to exhibit the beauty of grace in the lives of others. Keep in mind the truth of the following verse that "Above all, keep loving one another earnestly, since love covers a multitude of sins" (1 Peter 4:8, ESV).

My friends and family feel threatened by my new faith. How do I reassure them I care just as much for them?

When someone comes to Christ, a desire is created within to do all things to honor (recognize that God is God and we are not; also show our gratitude for His goodness, generosity and grace) God, to offer oneself as an instrument to God's greatness, generosity, and goodness and to worship God. Now the degree with which we do this and what that looks like will be different in each individual. Some may come right out of the doors totally committed and on fire for Christ, while for others, the changes and results of those changes may occur at a completely different and gradual pace over time. Yet, there will be some change and, as a result, others are bound to notice and may react with things like: "You're one of those religious nuts now, huh!" "That may be fine for you, but don't bring it around me because I do not need it!" "Too good for us now, huh!" "What's wrong with you, we have always hung out like this!" What you hear may cause you hurt and bring you pain because it seems like friends are not wanting anything to do with you. You think you're still the same person, but to others, you're not. And they are right.

You do not want to abandon your friends. You have found a new and better way of life and want so much for your friends to "get it," to see the same truth and come to Jesus. They may even tell you that you do not care for them any more. The reality is — you may indeed care more, as now you desire to tell them of the One who can give them real life.

So remember three things:

1) God is always at work!
2) Share your story in three easy points: What my life was like before, what happened when I committed myself to Jesus, and now this is my life. You do not need to be "qualified" or know how to quote God's Word from memory.

3) The best way to share God's love is not to tell them what **they** are doing wrong, but to live as an example of God's love and grace.

As you grow in Christ, study God's Word so that you become a craftsman who can better share the Word of God with others. In learning to live in your new identity as a child of God, it will always be important to treat others not how you used to treat them, but by the grace that God offers them, right where they are.

Now that I am a Christian should I feel different or see a difference in my life?

Before you became a Christian, while you may or may not have been a good person, you could do nothing to bring glory and honor to God. You could not even choose to live as though God existed. All you could choose was to live in a way that took you from one pleasure, comfort and approval by another. You probably did not even have a desire to do so. Ephesians 2:1-3 expresses the reason for this as "In the past you were dead because you sinned and fought against God. You followed the ways of this world and obeyed the devil." Your best works and efforts to God were nothing more "than a filthy rag" (Isaiah 64:6).

We are spiritually dead, not able to understand or comprehend the things the Bible says or anything really about God, himself. This is not how we were created and as a result that entire part of us is considered dead. Now because of our condition what might be in our eyes acts to pacify an angry God are nothing more than ratty, filthy rags.

Now that you know Christ as your Savior you will probably have different interests. You will have a desire to glorify or worship God. At first you may just find yourself reading the Bible or looking forward to going to church to worship God. Know that this is a sign of change and that you now have the ability to not only think Godward, but a desire to be in community with others who have also accepted Christ as their Saviour. It is also a sign that you are also choosing to make choices through the Holy Spirit enabling you that represent the work God is doing in giving you new abilities to serve Him and bring Him glory. New abilities through the Holy Spirit to think about the truths of the gospel and the Bible as the Holy Spirit helps you to do so. These actions will result in the ability to act in ways you could not before which will show others the passionate love of God and His grace. This may occur right away or slowly begin to appear as changes in your life.

As these changes occur in your life you will soon be able
to bear fruits (actions, thoughts, words) that are a result of the
Holy Spirit's work in your life. This is "the fruit of the Spirit: love,
joy, peace, patience, kindness, goodness, faithfulness, gentleness,
self-control; against such things there is no law" (Galatians 5:22-
23, ESV). This is in contrast to the works of the flesh (the ways
we used to think, act and speak that were based on the choices
we once made) which are "immoral ways, filthy thoughts, and
shameful deeds. They worship idols, practice witchcraft, hate
others, and are hard to get along with. People become jealous,
angry, and selfish. They not only argue and cause trouble, but they
are envious. They get drunk, carry on at wild parties, and do other
evil things" (Galatians 5:19-21). So as you can see there should
be a clear difference in how you lived before you came to Christ
and how you should live now that you are the Bride of Christ.
(Ephesians 5: 25-27 compares our relationship to Christ to the
relationship a husband and wife share.)

The above verse mentions one of the gifts of the Spirit being joy. The gift of joy is a direct gift that comes from the Holy
Spirit and is different than happiness. Happiness is based on
what our circumstances happen to be at the moment and joy is
present irregardless of our circumstances. Joy comes from living
life as one was designed to, in worship of the creator and as an
instrument of his glory. There is no greater joy for those who are
the bride of Christ than finding their mission and purpose in
being committed to the mission of making Christ known and
God glorified through serving others.

This is what we were designed for and what God intended
for us to do as He "created [us] in Christ Jesus for good works,
which God prepared beforehand, that we should walk in them"
(Ephesians 2:10, ESV). This joy, passion and mission is what
drove Paul to endure the things he describes in (2 Corinthians
11:24 -30) and "to count all things loss but to know Christ"
(Philippians 3:8, ESV). It is the work of the Holy Spirit in our
lives to bring truths to our mind of the Bible to mind (John
14:26), and to build strength with in us, which He does through

the grace of God as He gives us the power to live this new life that will often sustains us through deep periods of dark nights. At those times when joy seems ridiculous but God's Spirit is still there, never abandoning us.

Desire that your life count for something great! Long for your life to have eternal significance. Want this! Don't coast through life without a passion.[*]

---

[*] John Piper, *Don't Waste Your Life*. Crossway, 2003, p. 46.

Will coming to Jesus make my life easier or make me happy, healthy and wealthy?

There are two distinct errors often taught by speakers, teachers, and pastors, especially those on television, radio and the web:

1) The Christian life will solve all my problems and help me have the life I have always wanted.
2) Ask anything in Jesus' name and He will give it, whether it is health, wealth or general happiness.

There is a foundational error with both of these views. That foundational error being that it takes a work of God, namely salvation, and makes it about us.

This is an error because we see in Isaiah 48:9-11, God saying four times that "it is for His purpose that he has done these things." God will "place within us a new spirit and a new heart" (Ezekiel 36:26,38). He will do this so that we and others will know that **He** is God. It is "to the praise of His glory" He has saved us through His grace" (Ephesians 2:7).

Therefore, we must primarily always remember that the work of salvation is a work that He does for Himself. He does it because of His great love (Ephesians 2:4) and brings **His** creation back to **Him,** so they can praise **Him** and **His** greatness, goodness, and generosity can be showcased. He has not done this so that we can ask for more, expect more or demand more.

If we truly understand our condition before Christ and now realize that He has indeed rescued us, we will find in Him all we need, desire or want.

Will we notice a difference when we come to Christ? The first change that will most assuredly be noticed is a desire to begin to worship God. We will have a desire to pray and spend time in God's Word. And then we also have a desire to start living in a way that honors God. One thing that you can count on is that if you have placed your faith in Christ, you will notice differences somewhere. And with those differences will come other changes in your life and those changes may sometimes appear to bring difficulties or cause hardships. In fact because of some of the changes you will experience you will know that you have gone from being Satan's friend to his enemy. So expect, attacks, trials, and other hardships as Satan and his demons work to keep you from making choices honoring God and living in obedience (doing the things God wants).

God's process of making us like Christ is one that will stretch you and sometimes it will seem like life has become incredibly difficult. 1 Peter 4:12 says, "do not be surprised when trial comes that will test your faith." Paul in Philippians 1:29 said that "it has been granted to us for the sake of Christ to suffer." James, in 1:2-4 said "to count it all joy when we encounter various trials for the testing of our faith brings about steadfastness which will make sure we are complete lacking nothing."

So as you can see the Christian life will definitely have suffering and trials. As a result of those trials, the life we have may never look like the life we have always wanted. Also, quite likely everyday will not seem like Happy Hour or will we always be healthy and wealthy. This is the Christian life and we should not feel like we are doing something wrong because trials come. We may realize our desires have changed, and that we now want to become more like Christ. Even in the midst of such trials and suffering we can be assured that it will all work for our best (Romans 8:28). It really is for our best to be changed in a way that will enable us to live as we were originally designed and created to live. Which was to reflect God's character, to worship Him and to be used by Him to touch the lives of others with His grace, mercy and love.

As far as praying in Jesus' name and receiving whatever we want because Christ said "if you ask anything in my name" (John 14:14), no, it does not mean the Father will bless all requests or all things we may like or desire. Teaching like this often does not lead us to Christ but away from Him. Prayers that lead to developing an intimacy with God are those which increase within us a desire to worship **Him**, or make it about Him and not us are ones that God eagerly awaits to answer. When we pray to be used as greater instruments of God's glory, those requests the Father will unfailing and over abundantly give us.

We need to always remember that God is a God who brings life out of death and Christ showed us that real power comes from giving up control and letting Him have the power. Jesus challenged the rich young ruler and told the disciples that those who give it all away to follow Him would get it back in eternity, not here (Matthew 19:16-30). We must always remember that it is through deep suffering that God brought freedom through the tomb. As such often it will be through suffering that He will indeed show us the way to joy and freedom.

So don't be surprised if instead of getting healthier, wealthier and happier you instead come to the same point Paul did when he said, "Nothing is as wonderful as knowing Christ Jesus my Lord. I have given up everything else and count it all as garbage. All I want is Christ" (Philippians 3:8).

That does not mean that we should not pray for our needs, the needs of others, or bring every care, concern, burden, weight of life, the pains of everyday living to God. For He is indeed a Father who knows how to give good gifts (Matthew 7:11), One of those gifts He has given us is the ability to cry to Him like we would our earthly father with such things (Romans 8:15). We have been instructed to bring every care to Him because He loves us (1 Peter 5:7). Not only that God is a good God who eagerly wants to show us that love through His generosity and goodness (Isaiah 30:8), which may or may be shown through material blessings. Sometimes it is shown through the comfort of friends, love of our brothers and sisters, comfort of His Holy Spirit (which is God living in us, which is a precious gift, of itself), the ability to now live as we were created to be, through His grace, which is the greatest gift we have been given. So never hesitate to pray because he eagerly awaits to love you. Yet, his answers may not always look how we want them to look as he answers in ways that bring us closer to Him and make us Christlike.

Does the Bible really say if two or more pray in agreement on anything, God will do it for them? Does this mean God will give us anything?

The Bible surely seems to say that.

> *I promise that when any two of you on earth agree about something you are praying for, my Father in heaven will do it for you.* (Matthew 18:19)

> *Delight yourself in the Lord, and he will give you the desires of your heart.* (Psalms 37:4, ESV)

> *Beloved, I wish above all things that thou mayest prosper and be in health, even as thy soul prospereth.* (3 John 1:2, KJV)

> *Good people become wealthy.* (Proverbs 15:6)

> *And if they obey, they will be successful and happy from then on.* (Job 36:11)

So is the Bible promising us prosperity? Is it saying if I live a righteous life then I will be prosperous? Some would even teach that sickness is evil and as a result, sickness is from the Devil and we in fact sin when we say God is responsible for sickness. Are those teachings right?

As with all Scripture we must make sure that when we are forming our interpretation that it does not put us in conflict with other passages. Often these verses are taught to say such things as "we are not to be sick" or "while living here we should always prosper." Do such statements contradict or conflict with other verses in the Bible? Does God mean something else when the Bible speaks of prosperity? Should each passage be looked at the same way, with the same meaning? Is God totally in authority in order that He not only permits, but designs all things and as a result controls all things? Are there other reasons for sickness or suffering in poverty? Are there other passages which shed light on an understanding of these passages? What is the purpose of the Bible? Should we interpret verses by each passage or by the Bible as a whole, jointly fit together?

All of these are questions we must ask ourselves every time we hear this type of teaching! Our failure to ask questions like these always leads to error, misinterpretation, and as a result, misapplication.

If we are to pursue blessings, for indeed a righteous man would have wealth, then we would surely find this one of Christ's pursuits, right? Yet Jesus said in Matthew 8:20 "the Son of Man doesn't have a place to call his own." And in Luke 12:15 He said, "one's life does not consist in the abundance of his possessions."

> *Don't store up treasures on earth! Moths and rust can destroy them, and thieves can break in and steal them.* (Matthew 6:19)

Does the Bible offer further insight about a life lived in the pursuit of things? Do the words of a man, who if alive today would still be the wealthiest, smartest man in the world, shed further light? After acquiring much wealth, prosperity and fame, this man still deemed it all foolishness? This was the assessment of King Solomon after chasing wealth and more in Ecclesiastes 2:1-11.

How would God feel about those who claim to be His children and yet who desire more, want more, seek more, and are not satisfied with **Him** and **Him** alone? Did God redeem us to **Himself** in order that He can give us more, or so that He can make life easy? Was that really the reason, or was it so that He might hold us up as **His** masterpiece to the praise of **His** glory? This might in turn require **Him** to make surgical cuts in our lives, sometimes without anesthesia, in order to hold us up as masterpieces.

What about sickness? Is sickness and ill health a thing of evil, or is there another purpose? Christ echoes the same sentiments in John 9:3, when He says. "Neither this man nor his parents sinned, but this happened so that the works of God might be displayed in him."

Solomon said in Ecclesiastes 7:13 (ESV), "Consider the work of God: who can make straight what He has made crooked?"

Wait?! God makes things crooked that are straight!? What is that all about?! I thought God only made things straight that **were** crooked. For this is the attitude of those who would say that sickness is evil and prosperity is a sign of righteous living.

Ecclesiastes 7:14 says, that God is not only responsible for the good times but the bad as well. Isaiah 45:7 God says He is responsible for happiness and sorrow. So if God is responsible for the good times and the bad, sickness and sorrow, how can we say someone is sinning or is not being obedient (doing what God says), enough or that they do have enough faith. Perhaps there is another reason why God does these things.

There is one more issue that arises when we say that "if we have enough faith" or "live in a way that pleases God enough." We have made it again all about **us, our** faith and **our** righteousness. We have become like the Pharisees who point fingers at those we think are not living up to or meeting the list of rules we feel that they should be. As we look at those lives we may not think they are as prosperous or healthy as they should be.

While we may not outwardly say it — then again, some of us really do not know how to **not** say such things — we often think, "What is wrong with them?" "They must be sinning." "They need to get their lives together!" — as we gaze with so-called discernment into the lives of **others**. We forget we ourselves will never be able to do the things God wants us to either perfectly or enough. God has given all of us Christ's ability to do the things God wants us to. So that now he sees the perfect obedience of Christ' and not our muddied attempts at obedience (2 Corinthians 5:21). We were once dead (separated from God) in our sins and the very faith we have, He has given us (Ephesians 2:1).

When we remember these things, our gaze becomes less critical of others and more aware of the grace He gives each of us equally. It really is and always will be about **God** and **His** purpose.

If we are growing in Christ then our prayers and the things we ask for are going to reflect that. We will be coming to the point of sacrifice. We will realize our chief aim is to glorify God and God readily awaits to bless and grant the prayers that glorify Him. When we pray together with two or more to God, we will always find **Him** ready to bless and honor those prayer requests.

Some may say that it would glorify God for us to be happy, healthy and wealthy. Sometimes that is true. God is often blessed by the success, happiness and wealth of someone. However, even in that case it is rarely because we asked for it, but because it is within **His** design and purpose. And the plan was designed long before we were born. Remember, **He** truly has planned our steps before us.

We need to always remember that God is far less interested in our standard of living than He is in our standard of character. He is interested in what must be done to bring us back to that purpose for which we were created. The reason we were created was to have communication with God, to praise Him for being God and to be His mouthpiece, feet and hands exhibiting His goodness, generosity, grace, love and mercy. So that one day He may present us to the praise of **His** glory! Christ showed us that life comes not from grabbing more but in dying to ourselves.

"The only bumper sticker that a Christian should have is that which says 'I hate my life.'" - Pastor David Lyles, *Connection Fellowship*. What a powerful statement and a reflection of one of the most powerful truths in the gospels. So powerful, it is mentioned in three of the gospels as Christ said, "If any of you want to be my followers, you must forget about yourself. You must take up your cross and follow me" (Matthew 16:24, Mark 8:34, Luke 9:23). When Christ spoke of dying to ourselves He was referring to us not living to pursue our interests, our own worldly gain, our selfish ambition, our desire to get things our way but to give up all of that. So that we instead could pursue those things that make most of Christ, that make Him the number one thing in our lives, that reflect to others the work He has done in our lives.

When we pray for something, it is usually for our benefit. When God answers prayer, it is for His benefit, which may or may not always appear to have our best in mind, as we perceive it.

The best, in our eyes, always involves easy, whereas our best, in God's eyes, always involves our becoming who we were created to be. Allowing us then to make choices, decisions and commit actions that show that the Holy Spirit is working through us to enable us to bring honor to God through our lives. This is the beauty of grace. A beauty which allows us not to look at suffering, pain, loss and hurts as the ending, but rather the beginning (Philippians 1:29). It is the beginning of our understanding of the sufferings of Christ and where we find the God's unmerited love for us is indeed life giving and heart transforming. We are returned back to the purpose for which we were created, to live in worship of the Beloved.

The gospel of grace teaches us the gravity of chasing things that lead to a smaller return. Choosing to serve something other than God is always smaller and will always end up bringing more pain in our lives. While the reality of truth is that a greater return comes from a life of sacrifice towards kingdom advancement.

When it comes to God's promises, they are not grab bags to claim to see what awaits, nor are they piñatas waiting to be busted open (tested) so that we can see what treats fall out of them. As we look and expect to see whether God will keep His promises and what goodies He has in store for us. They are meant to point us to deeper truths about God, Christ, The Holy Spirit, God's Word, and Man. They reveal the character of God and the lack in man. His promises are there, not to reveal to us the smörgåsbord of great life happenings, but rather to reveal that God is most pleased when we find our deepest passion in Him and that He does what pleases Him, which is always to glorify Himself. God is always doing that which brings focus to Himself, His attributes and His work. It is not egotistical for God to do this. Yet it would be sin for God to attribute glory, praise or worship to anyone other than Himself. This would be the very definition of idol worship, for there is no other God like God.

Remember that the Bible is a story, God's story. A story written to tell us of how He has created us, chased us, loved us, redeemed us unto Himself and is crazy about us. It is not a convoluted book of separate passages and meanings where verses say one thing that may contradict something else. When we read the Bible as a cohesive book, we are less likely to make mistakes in application and meaning.

Won't teaching grace this way create apathy and spiritual laziness?

When we realize that we were once hopeless, tied to the railroad tracks of eternal death, destined to spend eternity away from God, now the opposite is truer, because now we are the rescued. We now have hope; we are no longer condemned, and nothing can separate us from the love of God. We now are the chosen Bride of Christ (Revelation 19-21). It creates a desire within us to worship God and to offer our bodies as living sacrifices.

When you were a kid and broke the rules and your parents brought the hammer down, what sort of desires did it create within you? More than likely, this created not a desire to please your parents but rather a desire to rebel further, because it probably made you angry. You may have felt that your parents did not get it! Did they not see all the other things you were doing? Did they not know how hard you were trying? They may have made you feel that you never measured up or would ever be able to make them happy. So this frustrated you and possibly made you feel, "Why should I even bother?"

Now what happened when you knew you had blown it and your parents not only did not bring the hammer down, they gave you a great gift? Did this make you want to rebel more or go out and do something to make your parents look bad? More than likely, it made you feel you were being loved by your parents, which in turn, made you want to do good things for your parents. Right?

Most will tell you that after you're saved, if you do not obey God's voice, you may not be saved or, at the very least, God will bring down a whole wrath of discipline on you. They will try to use the Law as a way to motivate you to serve God.

While the Word of God does tell us that He disciplines those whom He loves (Hebrews 12:6), this must always be balanced with David's words in Psalms 103:10 when he said, "God doesn't punish us as our sins deserve." David gives the reason for this in verse 14 when he said, "because he knows we are made of dust." While God disciplines those He calls His children, He is not saying He dishes out punishment as a result of our failures, or lack of good deeds or our inability to please Him. Rather it is the result of His work, His process of remolding us. Much like an athlete will discipline himself to run a race so he can collect a prize (1 Corinthians 9:24), so the Father disciplines those who He calls His children, not because of them, but because of Him. Through His sanctifying work, God presents His children as a finished product, worthy of praise to Himself.

The greatest motivation is always love and when we realize that we are indeed the chosen Bride, the Beloved, it should create a desire within us where hopelessness once lived, a desire to offer our whole lives as living sacrifices (Romans 12:1).

Giving someone more rules, a better list, and telling someone how they ought to live, will never be a good enough motivation to inspire one to do all things to God's glory and to live as God's instruments. All that will do is make one realize that they do not measure up. Which in effect is why Paul said, "those that try to live in such a way are cursed" (Galatians 3:21). Then in 2 Corinthians 3:6 he said, "the law kills and the spirit gives life." One thing is for sure, if we are constantly trying to keep ourselves good, using the law, we will live more like we are dead than alive in Christ. Not only will we be living as though we are dead, we will more than likely be killing those around us.

If we live in a way in which, under our own strength, we are constantly trying to do what the Bible says we will always feel like a failure. If we live with the understanding that we already have God's approval and now we obey, not to get it, but to say thank you for loving us. We will always feel love and treasured by God. When we feel this way it will always spill into the lives of others. The answer is rarely pointing to the law, but to the why and the who. Some have said that they have met drunks who pointed to the cross. The issue with this is not found in correcting their drunkenness but in correcting their understanding of their condition without Christ. It is in helping them see that when God saw His own wrath, it was almost more than He (Jesus) could handle as a human in the garden. When Christ saw the abandonment of the Father that our sins would cost **Him**, it shook Him to the core and caused **Him** great despair. Yet, because it glorified the Father, He marched forward in order to give us, **His** Bride the most precious gift a bride has ever known.

The nails may have represented our sin but it was God's desire to show **His** exceeding riches towards us that kept **Him** on the cross. Now we have been given the most precious ring that a bride has ever been given. It's called **grace**. Until we can fully grasp those truths, lasting changes that lead to God's purpose and glory will rarely happen in us. We can never get a full grasp on how bad our sin is and how much God loves us. But the more we do grasp that, the more it compels us to lift our lives in praise and worship and in service.

This is what Paul meant when he said that, "We are ruled by Christ's love for us. We are certain that if one person died for everyone else, then all of us have died. [15]And Christ did die for all of us. He died so we would no longer live for ourselves, but for the one who died and was raised to life for us" (2 Corinthians 5:14-15).

This is the working out of our salvation that Paul speaks of in Philippians 2:11-13 that many love to uphold as proof that we do indeed need to do something. The question here is not, is it tough work focusing and reminding ourselves of the truths we just mentioned? It is indeed tough work requiring the discipline of an athlete.

We must never forget that the word salvation in our language deals with not only our justification (being saved from the penalty of our sin), but also our sanctification (being saved each day from the power of sin in our lives) and our glorification (one day being saved from the presence of sin). It is with our being saved from the daily power of sin in our lives that Paul is most concerned here, as he encourages those in the church at Philippi and us, in verse 11 to be obedient. In verse 13, he gives us not only the how, but the who, as he tells us that it is God who creates not only the will, but enables us to do so. Paul points us back to the ultimate servant and the sacrificed Lamb in Philippians chapters 1 and 2. It is by looking at Christ and the cross where Christ stated "It is finished" that we are able to live in such a way.

We do not focus on our obedience, our holiness, our being and doing more, but focus on the One who could. The truth of the matter is that we do not have to measure up, Christ already did. We are all failing, the sooner we realize this, the deeper our appreciation and understanding of God's grace will be. For it is not about our performance, but Christ's giving the ultimate performance. Nor is it about our ability to keep God's requirements, because we can't. It is about the One who could keep God's requirements.

So in truth the gospel of grace ought to be taught or preached in such a way that we believe that it is OK to live as we please, because God covered it all. This was Paul's fear when he finished Romans chapter 5. Yet the gospel also should be preached or taught so completely that it inspires us to choose to live to praise God in all things and to choose now to live as instruments of God's character and vessels of **His** glory, which was Paul's message in Romans 6. Keep in mind that an all-powerful God will continue to work in our lives until He is the most important thing to us. We will find our deepest passions and joy in living sacrificial lives to His glory. If we do not have some fear and trembling in our relationship with God then we have no knowledge of who God really is or that He refuses to share the spot that only He can and should fully occupy.

What is easy or cheap grace?

One often hears about "easy or cheap grace" from those who say, "If you preach grace without a focus on how we should be obedient or holy then you cheapen God's grace." Perhaps this may not be what you hear, maybe it will sound something like this "If you are always preaching grace you may give those listening the feeling they can go on sinning and thus make grace easy or cheap."

To say that we need to be careful of teaching grace without the law is indeed true, but it is also just as true to say that we need to be careful of teaching the law without grace. For it is not one without the other, but both together and individually, that needs to be taught.

Though we do not teach grace with the law so that we do not abuse grace because we always will. Rather, so that as grace teaches us, we know what it is teaching us (Titus 2:12) and enabling (2 Timothy 2:1) us to do. This is the reason why we should not teach the law without grace. For the law is not something that can be achieved, a standard to shoot for, something that we can hope to live. But if we do more and be more, then in effect we can achieve more, which pleases God with our obedience. None of us will ever be perfect without Christ. None of us can keep God's standard of perfection, which is why He has given us Christ's righteousness. Christ never sinned! But God treated Him as a sinner, so that Christ could make us acceptable to God (2 Corinthians 5:21). We can never really please God with our obedience because Matthew 5:48 says, "You therefore must be perfect, as your Heavenly Father is perfect." For the law to be anything less than perfect would make it something that it is not. When we make the law less than God's standard, as it describes His character of perfection, a different problem may arise. The problem may not be that we may or may not have made grace easy or cheap, but that we have possibly made the Law of God cheap. So that is why we should never teach the law without grace. For only grace enables us to live the law, otherwise we would be without the ability to do so.

Our ability to live in a way that honors God is not enabled through becoming more aware of God's laws, but through becoming more aware of the cost of the grace given freely to each of us and because of who God is. The Psalmist said the cost of God's favor upon men who could never do anything to deserve it was the ultimate cost, that there indeed is not a more costly gift (Psalms 49:7-9). John, in Revelation 3:18, compared our salvation to gold. The apostle Peter pointed out that our salvation is not purchased through any materialistic thing that we could provide or offer, but through precious blood of the Perfect Lamb (1 Peter 1:18-19). So yes, grace is costly, it cost Jesus his very life. Yet, He did not give His life so that He could be paid back, or so that one day we could collect our good deeds and try to prove ourselves worthy of the gift. If the gift of our salvation given through the death of Christ on the cross was dependent on how we responded, it would no longer be grace (Romans 11:6).

Nor would it represent God or could it come from God. As one of God's characteristics is that He is pure, man is anything but pure (Job 25:4). This would be like having the purest diamond in the world and then saying "OK! Let's cut it and it will be even purer." No, the minute the diamond is touched by human hands it will now have even more imperfections. God's grace is purer than any diamond, so if the value of it was dependent on man's ability to value such gift, or be responsible with such a gift, it would immediately become imperfect. That is why the value of grace must be from the giver, God. What was the cost value of such a gift, the very life of God himself when He took on the form of man (Jesus) and became obedient to death (Philippians 2:5-11).

This is why Christianity is different than any other religion. Every other religion has a system in place that shows us how to get to God. God says, "You cannot come close, no matter what you do, so I'm coming to you. Even if you could come close you still can't come, that horrible sin in your life I don't want it anywhere near me, it's like you looking at the most despicable, horrific thing you can imagine, even worse (Habakkuk 1:13). Not to mention that your best efforts to do what I ask of you, or to try to please me, or impress me, are to me like when you stepped in your neighbor's wild animal's mess, got it all over your shoes, smelled it, then tracked it in your house, and had to look at it all over your shoes and your floor. Remember how you felt, well that is still a smidgen of how such efforts make me feel (Isaiah 64:6). So I needed to provide a way that cost me immensely, not you." So to say that we must be responsible or live in such a way that we do not make grace cheap, or easy, or abuse it is a return to man's way of thinking. It reflects a misunderstanding of what our salvation truly costs, the character of God, and just how messed up we truly are."

Saying grace is absolutely free, or that it is not dependent on what we do, is easy to get (all we have to do is believe and receive) is not saying that it is cheap or easy. For it is not cheap to God, nor is it easy. For God to offer grace it always costs Him His mercy. Mercy extended to those who will never fully know how much they need it, or much less appreciate it. Mercy that offers, through the cross, protection from God's wrath.

To say that we can indeed do, we must do something so that grace is neither easy nor cheap; cheapens not only God's characteristics of mercy and grace, but also His wrath and His need for justice. Thus, in essence, by doing that we cheapen God, Himself. To think that we could be responsible with such mercy, so as to offer up pleasing works, is to say that God's wrath is not so severe. Yet, it was not the road to Calvary and what Christ was facing on that road (the beatings, torture, pain, humiliation and ultimately death) that caused Him to know fear and emotional distress, but facing the wrath of God head on. Imagine God encountered His own wrath as a human and it caused such turmoil in Him that He sweat drops of blood. This is what is known as "gospel truth" (that we are in desperate need of a savior. God who loves us deeply provided one at, no cost to us) that transforms.

Gospel truth is not just needed before we accept Christ as our savior. In fact it may be needed more after, or at the very least we come to understand it for what it is and the impact it is having in our lives. For before we came to Christ, nothing of God's word made sense to us (1 Corinthians 2:14). Now that we are in a relationship with God again, He has given us His Holy Spirit to point to, illuminate and remind us of the truths found in God word, **starting with gospel truth** (John 14:26).

The truths of that gospel do not change simply because we are now in Christ. Grace, while still costly, is still pure and as a result still given without any bearing on the recipient's response. The minute this stops being true, grace stops being a true gift from God and a representation of His character. Because His mercy stands in the pathway of His wrath so that He can offer grace, it will always be costly to God. Because it came at the sacrifice of the perfect lamb it will always have come through a difficult journey. Grace speaks of the passionate love of an Almighty God always given freely, no less now that you know Christ, than it did before. That is why such knowledge does not inspire one to go out and paint graffiti on walls screaming "God Is Dead!" but rather to shout joyfully with exuberance that God Is Indeed alive. Instead of accusing us of painting walls they may very well accuse us of sniffing the paint (Acts 2:15).

The more we grow to understand not only an Almighty, Creator of The Universe, Grace giving God, but how deeply He loves us and wants to shower us with grace, the greater our desire will be to live the law. Once we were the enemy of God (Romans 5:10), now we are the deeply desired ones of God, the apple of His eye (Psalm 17:8, ESV), His most excellent one (Psalm 16:3, ESV), and the ones He is passionate about. Such knowledge and understanding will rarely lead one to a life of lawlessness but rather to a deep form of gratitude. A gratitude that results in our becoming creative, excited and about finding new ways to tell His story and ours. To find our passion and mission in making God known, bringing Him glory shouting Praises to His name, in and with all that we do (1 Corinthians 10:31).

I recently saw a bumper sticker that read, "God loves you! But don't let it go to your head!" What's with that? Of course you should let it go to your head. If God loves you and it doesn't go to your head, you just haven't understood. If the God of the universe really likes you, that ought to put everything else into perspective. It should make you laugh and dance with great joy. It might even cause those who don't understand to say about you what they said about the apostles (see Acts 2:13) — that you are plastered.*

---

* Brown, Steve. *Three Free Sins: God's Not Mad at You*. Howard Books. 2012

What is the motivation upon which I should serve God?

Ever go to a zoo and watch how the animals seem very docile, even the wildest of creatures? If we were to see such animals in the wild, they indeed would be roaming free and running with unchained, uncaged abandonment. This is the difference between someone who is motivated to live their lives by something smaller than God (idolization) in order to gain the acceptance of man or God, versus someone who has discovered that God loves them regardless of how they respond or act.

For indeed, such freely given love and grace is a great motivator but not only a great motivator, but also a breath of fresh air as it allows its recipients to breathe the fresh air of freedom. Freedom from what? Freedom from the rejection of others, fear of failure, need for approval from others to make us feel good about ourselves; or the need to find comfort, happiness and relief from things that are smaller than God. Freedom to what? Freedom to run, freedom to be wild, adventurous, creative. The freedom to dance even if they look at you with contempt (2 Samuel 6:16), and to sing even if others tell you to "please be quiet you're hurting my ears" (Psalm 104:33). Most of all, freedom to be as we were created to be. We were created to be reflections of the glory of God (Genesis 1:26-27, 1 Corinthians 4:16), to worship Him (praise Him for being God and nothing else, [Psalm 29:2, Psalm 40:3]) and to make Him known (Romans 15:9).

Trapped by cages made of idols (anything that we seek—security, pleasure, comfort, approval from, that is not God) that we have built in our lives and the chains that are attached to each of these cages. Chains like our need for a stress-free life, our need for the approval of others (to be liked by others, to have others think well of us, to be pleased with who we are and what we do), needing to make sure that everything is in it's place or in order. This is just a small list of the chains that are attached to those cages. What is even worse is that some of these cages (remember made by our idols) have the appearance of being a good thing, and in truth, some of them are (good things can be idols). Sometimes it is not just the cages that we work hard to maintain and keep clean and respectable that are the problems, but that these things become the reason we exist, our focus in life, why we live. The need to maintain these cages becomes the motivation of our lives.

Through grace, offered through Christ, we are offered freedom from these cages. Like most animals that have been trapped in captivity for long, or who have been severely injured (sin injures us, and why the old man must be put to death and why we are given new faculties), we have become docile and no longer know how to handle such freedom. So, we look for things to keep the freedom in check, in perspective, in effect such freedom scares us. So, we start looking for the cage that once seemed so comfortable, easy and controllable. So, instead of God's love and grace becoming our motivation for living for God, we turn back to the old familiar ways either through sin (continuing living in the same old lifestyle, making the same choices, maintaining the same cages) or through looking for motivation through living God's laws in our strengths. Anything not done in faith is sin (Hebrews 11:6). It is faith that we have been redeemed, set free and no longer have to live for approval or acceptance because we already are. Trying to gain God's approval, or acceptance, or attempting to be deserving of His loving grace is not only a form of legalism (living by standards in order to get acceptance of God's or anyone else's), but is also just forming a different kind of cage, and creating an image of a god who does not exist (Which is making an idol, little gods). Doing this seemingly controls our freedom and makes sure that we are responsible and not abusive with it, but the real problem is this robs us of the joy that comes from being saved and more than likely will bleed into others and rob theirs as well. Living becomes laborious and we are unable to exhibit the joy that comes from knowing we are passionately loved by God.

So how do we break free into the freedom God has called to, and not continue to be trapped by the small cages? How do we learn how to truly be captivated, motivated by God's love and grace? What does such motivation look like and how does it pour out of us to be infectious into the lives of others so that they find God not a taskmaster, but a God who delights in them (Psalm 100:2)?

Where our cages demand we serve them and as a result the need to do so becomes our motivating factor? God does not need, nor is He served through the deeds we do (Acts 17:24-26). He really has called us to freedom and it is no longer a question of what comes next, or what do we need to do to keep God happy with us, but **WHY**? Since nothing can bring a charge against us and the reasons for shame and for why we need to put up defenses are gone. Now, nothing can ever stand before us and point fingers at us to tell us of how we are failing, why do we need to do anything (Romans 8:1, 34)? This brings us full circle and back to the original question. Paul answered it beautifully in 2 Corinthians 5:14-15.

> We are ruled by Christ's love for us. We are certain that if one person died for everyone else, then all of us have died. And Christ did die for all of us. He died so we would no longer live for ourselves, but for the one who died and was raised to life for us.

We live for the One who brought us life, who opened the cages, who gave us freedom by giving up His own life (Isaiah 61:1). Because it is not demanded of us, nor is the grace of God dependent on how we respond, our motivation becomes one of deep gratitude because He loved us first regardless of whether we loved Him back again (1 John 4:19).

He did not open the cages so that we could just move from one to another. Rather, so that we might serve wanting nothing. Love in a way that truly exhibits God's love even if we are never loved back. We can now take risks without needing a safety net to ensure that everything stays safe and secure. Able to give till our pockets have holes in them. Individually we can leave the comfort of what we knew to be familiar to experience what is totally foreign to us (starting with grace). Now we can seek others interests at the expense of even our pleasure and place others first even when getting close makes a cactus seem soft. Not to mention we can forgive when doing so seems like someone just gave us a root canal. Our responses to others are seasoned with the love and mercy of God, even when it feels someone is pushing the rusty nail in our foot even deeper.

Paul would tell us how we do this when he told us in Romans 12:2 "Do not be conformed to this world, but be transformed by the renewal of your mind, that by testing you may discern what is the will of God, what is good and acceptable and perfect." So how do we learn to be motivated in such a way? Moment by moment renewing our mind (Ephesians 4:23). How does such renewing occur? Here is how it does not occur; by creating a new cage made up of the laws we feel are important to keep. It occurs as we spend time in God's word (Romans 10:17) and the Holy Spirit reminds us, illuminates for us and points us to new truth (John 14:26), new truth found in the gospel of grace (God loves us even when we could not love ourselves or were worthy to be loved, sent Christ to die for us, redeemed us and made us His). As the Holy Spirit does this it allows the chains to fall, the cage walls to be destroyed, so that our focus becomes the One who not only started our story, is currently writing it, but will finish it (Hebrews 12:2). Through the Holy Spirit's work the cages we could not see become visible and the lies we once believed become seen for what they are and Satan is no longer able to blind us (2 Corinthians 4:4).

As our eyes are opened to who God really is, how passionately in love with us He is and how much grace He has given us, we become more aware of who we were once, how we lived, the choices we made, the cages that kept us trapped and for the first time we discover real freedom and the ability to enjoy that freedom. We realize though that to not offer our bodies back to God is not just the least we can do, but is the only motivation that there can be for being obedient to the things God asks of us. His law we find great delight in (Romans 7:22) as we realize anything else robs us of this freedom and just places us back in the cage (Romans 12:1).

I have been told I need to make myself more deserving of God's grace. Is this true?

There really is only one reply to this. "We are not deserving of grace, plain and simple!" No amount of effort, focus on obedience, focus on our holiness, focus on anything we might think we can do will ever qualify us to receive grace. How about this for a mind blowing concept; we already are as qualified, as we can be. Not only to receive grace, but to receive the inheritance God has waiting for those Christ calls His Bride (Colossians 1:12-14, ESV)! It is absolutely impossible for anyone who has accepted God's gift of grace and thus become a child of God to not abuse, misuse or be irresponsible with God's gift of grace.

While we cannot make ourselves more deserving of grace, we can choose or not choose to say thank you by how we live. This is a freedom we never had before. Yet, even in this we do not make such choices to be deserving of grace, to retain grace (God's favor and strength) or to be responsible with grace. For even those very choices are empowered by God through His grace (Colossians 1: 11, ESV). Not only are they empowered by God through His grace, if they are not made in faith then it is sin (Romans 14:23, ESV). Faith that God is no longer judging us by how we live, whether we are deserving of grace or not, whether we are being responsible with His grace, but by the fact that Christ became our sin and as a result we are now viewed through Christ's perfect obedience, not our inability to obey God's laws (everything the Bible tells us to do) (2 Corinthians 5:21).

If we could be deserving of grace, then it would no longer be grace (Romans 11:6) because grace is the favor of God freely given to those who deserve nothing but His wrath. Given not because they could pick themselves up in such a way as to gain His pleasure, but because they never could. Given out of the mercy and love of God so that one day he might show the goodness of His grace (Ephesians 2:7). In fact, not only were we not deserving of it, we did not even desire it. All we desired was to live life like every day was Mardi Gras (Ephesians 2:3). So now to think that we might make ourselves more deserving is to think we can change who we naturally are. If we came to this walk of grace through grace then we must continue on this journey through that same grace (Galatians 3:3-5). God is not making us into who we were created to be because we are obedient. God is making us into who we were created to be because Christ was obedient. As He is remaking us we are enabled to be obedient through the Holy Spirit working through us (1 Peter 2:5).

Grace is freely given and flows to us, not out of some ability of our own to pursue holiness (a way of life pleasing to God). No, it is given because One was holy (already pleased God). This is why we are now free (Romans 3:24), and there no longer exists any condemnation (penalty of God's wrath and justice) for those who are in Christ Jesus (Romans 8:1, 34). Shame no longer has the ability to make us feel as though we need to hide our failures because of our failure to live in a way to please God. Unless we choose to allow it to have that power. That is why it is not about how we are changing, how we are climbing some mountain of spiritual achievement, or how far we have come. For when we make it about those things, we will surely somewhere take credit for that which Christ does for us (Galatians 2:19-21). That does not mean we sit idly by or passively by while Christ goes "Will you move out of the way?" No, it means that we should be (though we have the freedom not too) aggressive in making daily choices that reflect our new identity (children of God, the reflection of God, the bride of Christ) and a heart of gratitude, it is never in our strength that those choices are made. God enables us to make those choices now, each day (Philippians 2:13).

That is why it is important, moment by moment, to remind ourselves of the truth of the gospel of grace and the love God has toward each one of us, so we might make those choices for the right reasons. Yet, even when we fail to make those right choices, and probably only about 10% of the time will we make the right ones, God's grace covers it. We confess our failures and accept the forgiveness that awaits for us (1 John 1:9). We do not confess to get, because even here we could not do it in such a way to deserve it but because it has already been given and we merely accept that which is waiting for us. He eagerly awaits to wrap His loving arms around us.

If we could make ourselves more deserving, then we could surely claim the right to stand before God, present our achievements and record books that we have kept, and possibly claim the right to do so. Paul said, "God has laid such arguments to rest." In Ephesians 2:9, Paul said, "It isn't something you have earned, so there is nothing you can brag about." Not that we would have enough to brag on anyway. We have more in common with Paul than we would like to admit as we struggle just to daily live out our new identity as one of God's chosen children (Romans 7:18). Rather than doing the things that will make us useful, more often than not we do not and end up being the ones that Peter spoke of in 2 Peter 1:9, who "have forgotten that your sins are forgiven." That is why we can be thankful every day is a new day in which we are not only taught by grace (Titus 2:11-12, ESV) in how to make choices out of our new identity, but empowered by grace to do so (2 Timothy 2:1, ESV). Choices not to serve ourselves, but to worship God and serve others, not so that we might become more deserving of His love, but because He loved us first.

So now we obey what the Bible tells us we should do. We should, as long as the motivation is gratitude and not to get something we already have, God's approval. Our tendency, though, will always be to do such things to seek the approval of God and others. We are like defense attorneys constantly trying to defend why we are indeed failing, or working to cover up that we are failing. We hope that, if others see (or at least think) we are getting it right, instead of our failures, they will respond with approval. When we try to impress others and God, God in turn must go, "it's not about you!" In fact, the first step toward learning to accept that it is about Christ and not us, is to stop trying to present evidence to others that we are okay (2 Corinthians 3:4-5). The truth is we are not okay. When we stop trying to convince ourselves that we are being responsible with God's grace, we will actually be enabled to receive God's new grace offered each day (James 4:6).

In a world where there are no free fliers, where everything is built around reward points, where one is judged by how together one can keep it together, grace is indeed a foreign concept. Grace breaks the approval trap, busts it wide open. As it says you already are accepted (Romans 15:7) and deeply loved, it daily reminds us that we already are the excellent ones of God (Psalms 16:3, ESV). **Grace** brings a freedom to choose, not to become more deserving, because we can't. Instead it allows us to choose to live in our new identity, bearing the fruits of such identity or to choose not to (Galatians 5:16-22). Yet, as we choose not to we are not choosing freedom, but slavery again. A slavery that keeps us thinking and living, not by our new identity, but by our old. In doing so, we cannot enjoy being the deeply desired ones of God, for we are still looking for approval in much smaller things than God. Living in such a way will only bring frustration, heartache and disappointment. When we choose to live as a special one to God, and instruments of God (1 Peter 2:9), it not only allows us to live in the freedom found through grace, but to be an instrument of grace to others.

God's grace makes the lazy worker who shows up at closing time with his hand out expecting the same pay as the one who has sweated in the hot sun all day, deserving of the same pay (Matthew 20:1-16). It just does not call those who were the wedding party's invited guests, but those who are homeless on the streets just as deserving to be at the party (Matthew 22:1-14). It makes the one who teased, threw rocks, hired others to bully and murder those believing in Christ a valuable tool in God's kingdom (Acts 8:3, 9:1, 22:20). This is the radicalness of grace and why, no matter how hard we try, we can never make ourselves as bad as what we once were, walking dead (Ephesians 2:1). Grace really does allow us to enjoy being in a relationship with the Creator of the universe, not because we could ever be responsible with or deserve to be in such a relationship, but because Christ already was.

So, if you are trying to make yourself deserving, stop. If you're wondering if you can be responsible with it, you can't. If you're asking others to be or do something they cannot do, then you're living more with Peter Pan in the land of Make Believe than you are with Christ in the reality of being His wonderful chosen Bride!

I think good preachers should be like bad kids. They ought to be naughty enough to tiptoe up on dozing congregations, steal their bottles of religion pills … and flush them all down the drain. The church, by and large, has drugged itself into thinking that proper human behavior is the key to its relationship with God. What preachers need to do is force it to go cold turkey with nothing but the word of the cross-and then be brave enough to stick around while [the congregation] goes through the inevitable withdrawal symptoms.[*]

---

[*] Capon, Robert. *The Foolishness of Preaching: Proclaiming the Gospel Against the Wisdom of the World.* Wm. B. Eerdmans Publishing Company. First Edition. 1997.

Can I get more of God's grace?

This question may or may not seem to be from an attitude that brings another question which is, "As I grow in my walk of grace and I become more obedient to God or holy (More like God), will God give me more grace?"

Paul said in, Ephesians 1:3, "Blessed be the God and Father of our Lord Jesus Christ, who has blessed us in Christ with every spiritual blessing in the heavenly places" (ESV). So Paul states, without exception, that we have been given all spiritual blessings through and in Christ Jesus. Peter expresses this same truth in 2 Peter 1:3 when he says "We have everything we need to live a life that pleases God. It was all given to us by God's own power, when we learned that He had invited us to share in His wonderful goodness." So with the words of Peter we see that we indeed have been given everything we need to live this Christian life. So we already have all of God's grace. Not only that, but we can be confident that God gives us the fullness of all of those blessings every day (Lamentations 3:23).

Because grace is not only a gift, but the single most quality in which we see the expressive hand of God at work in our lives; we know that it is pure. Since it speaks loudest of who God is it must indeed be pure, or it could not represent, nor be a gift from God. Because we are not pure (Job 25:4), our hands or our deeds cannot be mixed up with grace, otherwise grace would no longer be pure and as a result it would cease to be grace (Romans 11:6, ESV). So grace is always given freely to those who, not only don't deserve it, but cannot deserve it. Not only do we not deserve it, we do not even know we need it, before we come to Christ (Ephesians 2:1-3). Imagine tomorrow a child is getting ready to stick their hand in the light socket and before they do their parent stops them by grabbing their hands. The child does not know they needed to have their hands grabbed, they only know they did not get to do what they wanted to do which causes them to throw a fit and scream but "**I want to touch!**" This is, in a very minute way, an example of what God does through both

His common and His transforming, saving grace. He prevents us, even when we do not know it, from making a choice that could quite possibly injure us. He not only does this for those He has brought back into a relationship with Him, He does this for all of mankind. These actions are always given regardless of whether the one who benefits from it is deserving of it are not.

So because grace is pure, regardless of our reactions, or how we respond to it, it truly is God's favor on us even when we do not deserve it. Given when we did not even know we needed it to save us from certain death (eternal separation from God). So now there are no actions in which we can do or not do to make us more deserving or less deserving of God's amazing grace. So we can believe God's word when it says we have all spiritual blessings, everything we need to live this life we live now empowered by God through Christ (Colossians 1:11).

We have all we need, but that does not mean that we are using all we have. It is often not that we get more of God's grace (we just saw this is not true), but that we are able to use more of His grace. So what keeps us from using every bit of grace God gives us? In short, pride (James 4:6). Because we continue to seek the approval of others. Because other's opinions matter more to us than the Word of God we will often put up fronts, layers, become our own defense attorneys in order to keep others from seeing how we are failing to live in a way that pleases God or others. We are afraid to admit that we are failing at living in a way that brings honor to God, because we fear the rejection of others. Rather, instead, we hold up our little lists of things that we are doing right, how we are getting it right, rather than how we are getting it wrong. We hold up what we think we are doing right, while we jump quickly to criticize, attack and point out the faults of others. This always makes us feel better about ourselves.

We are the parent who keeps their child in line at the restaurant rather than running wild like the other children. We are the husband who remembers every anniversary and birthday and who never works too much while our friends are total idiots. We are the wives and mothers who keep the perfect home, always

makes sure our children are properly dressed and our husband's
lunches are perfectly packed. We worry and overwork trying to
please those we love. Not because we want to serve them, but
because how we feel about ourselves depends on their pleasure
with us. We stress ourselves out over making sure that we are
indeed reading our Bible faithfully and having those consistent
quiet times (not that we should not do that, but it should not be
done in a way in which it becomes a source of approval).

So we labor, sweat, kick ourselves when we fail and fail to
experience the joy of our salvation. There really is great joy to be
found in knowing we have been delivered from shame and the
need to perform to be accepted, because we already are by God.
Yet, we never experience this joy that comes because we're still
busy trying to keep it together and trying to keep others from
knowing that we are complete failures. When we do this we
place something else in our lives in which we get approval from.
In doing so, we say that something smaller than God is more
important, and as a result we get lost in the sins of idol worship
and pride as we serve not only that smaller thing but also others
as we work to get them to notice us. Idol worship will always
keep us from experiencing God's grace because we are refusing
to take God at His word when He said "I love you, you need do
nothing else." Instead we let that idol tell us how we should feel
about ourselves. (Idol worship is when we find comfort, security,
or pleasure from something smaller or another source than God.
For only God can really give us, these things.)

Yet even here, while we make something smaller more important than God, God responds to us in grace. This does not
mean His response will not be painful, for anytime God has to
remove something we are holding tightly onto it always is painful, this is called Godly discipline (Hebrews 12:6). Which He
always does because He loves us, wants what is best for us and
always does through His grace (1 Corinthians 15:10). Imagine
the three year old whose parent rips the item out of his hand
that he so badly wanted. At that moment the three year old is
not thinking good thoughts towards the parents nor is he at all

happy. We will feel the same way when God removes that thing we have been holding tightly to because He loves us too much to allow us to settle for anything but Him. When we settle for such a thing it is always sin and grace always is given large so that it brings us to the point that God becomes first again (Romans 5:20). So it is not that we have gotten more of God's grace but that we indeed have experienced more.

The same pride that keeps us working to keep from admitting failure, keeps us from humbling ourselves so that we might experience more of God's grace. As long as we keep working to not be seen as failures we will not be able to fully grasp the grace that God so lovingly awaits to give us. The more we admit how much of a failure we really are, the more we not only will be able to appreciate God's grace, but the more we will experience it to its fullest. This is what we see Paul expressing to Timothy in, 1 Timothy 1:15, "The saying is trustworthy and deserving of full acceptance, that Christ Jesus came into the world to save sinners, of whom I am the foremost" (ESV). Paul was no longer concerned with putting up a front, but rather instead joyfully admits "I'm a failure!" In doing so he is able to fully experience the grace of God.

So we do not get more of God's grace by doing more, but quite the opposite. As we stop trying to make ourselves something we cannot make ourselves (we cannot make ourselves sinless). We stop trying to keep others from seeing that we are failures and admit that we are indeed a big failure. It is then that we are able to experience more of God's grace. As we experience more of God's grace it enables us to live in a way that says thank you for loving me even when I did not know I needed Your love, deserved Your love and for continuing to love me even though I fail more than I get it right. Which has the reciprocal effect of making us feel like we are getting more grace.

> Now we find in ourselves a strength which is not
> our own, and which is freely given to us whenever we
> need it, raising us above the Law, giving us a new law

which is hidden in Christ: the law of His merciful love for us. Now we no longer strive to be good because we have to, because it is a duty, but because our joy is to please Him who has given all His love to us! Now our life is full of meaning!*

---

*   Thomas Merton, *Seasons of Celebration: Meditations on the Cycle of Liturgical Feasts*. Ave Maria Press. 2009.

Will my being faithful help build, sustain, or maintain my identity in Christ?

A despondent Prince Hamlet in the opening of the "Nunnery Scene" in Shakespeare's play *Hamlet* utters these words "**To be, or not to be...**" as the pains of life have beat him up and he ponders whether it is even worth living. We would echo this and say that this really is the question each individual who has chosen Christ as His savior must make to live as Christ's or not. To live for Christ or not. To live as one of God's chosen special instruments or not. Except if we choose the "not to be" we choose a life of utter madness.

Choosing not to live as one who believes that Christ has indeed risen from the dead is no choice at all. For if Christ has not risen from the dead then living for Christ means Paul was right when he said those who do are to be absolutely pitied. Indeed we will find ourselves in the same place Hamlet found himself in feeling utter despair (1 Corinthians 15: 20-24).

Yet, Christ Is Risen Indeed (Luke 24:34)! Because of this we indeed do have hope, not only hope but a promised inheritance (Hebrews 9:15-17). For we have been given an inheritance that is "imperishable, undefiled, and unfading, kept in heaven" (1 Peter 1:4). We have also been given a new identity, not through our own old abilities, but through the death, burial and resurrection of the Perfect Lamb (Jesus). Learning to live in this new identity has a direct bearing on how faithful we are but our faithfulness does not have a bearing on our identity. In other words, while we should be faithful because we have been given a new identity, our identity is not based on any faithfulness of our being or doing. Rather, it is a faithfulness built on the back of Christ, not ours. It was His back upon which the stripes (Christ was beat with a whip on the way to the cross) of our sin were laid (Isaiah 53:5). His blood purchased our new identity (1 Peter 1:19).

If our identity in Christ was dependent on our response, actions, or our faithfulness then Peter could not possibly have been right. For the minute we could bear one bit of responsibility for such an identity it would become nothing better than something perishable, it would be defiled and as such would surely not be lasting. However, knowing who we are in Christ allows us to know how deeply we are loved, treasured, how valuable we are and how much grace (favor) we have been given (Psalm 103:3-4). As the reality of our identity now in Christ becomes more real to us, it frees us to come out of the cages that we have made through our need to keep up appearances, remain secure, be comfortable, be in control, and seek to please ourselves. Only then can we move to a greater freedom and choose to live with a heart of gratitude for that new identity (John 8:32).

For our identity now in Christ lets us know that we no longer need to be in control to be somebody. We no longer need to be comfortable to feel good about ourselves. Security no longer has the same meaning. Our security is not based on what we accomplished or what we have, but what Christ did and as a result what He has given us (Ephesians 1:6-7). Our approval no longer comes from the lips of others but from the words of God (Colossians 1:12). As a result, because of our identity we now can love, serve and give with no thought to how the recipient responds. That is called grace and we now can be bearers of grace because we received it first.

As we become free and walk further away from the cages that used to confine us, we learn to discover our mission and purpose in life through that new identity. For we understand that the greatest treasure we have is the relationship that now gives us our new identity and is the reason for which we now should live. As we learn to live according to our identity now as a child of Almighty God (John 1:12), a royal priest (1 Peter 2:9), a chosen child of God (Colossians 3:12), a member of Christ's body (1 Corinthians 12:27), a vessel of God's grace and glory (2 Corinthians 4:7), the bride of Christ (Ephesians 5:25), friends of Christ (John 15:15), a citizen of heaven (Philippians 3:20), hidden with Christ in God (Colossians 3:3), holy and blameless (Ephesians 1:4), a saint (Ephesians 1:18), adopted by God (Ephesians 1:5), a worker for and with God (2 Corinthians

6:1), a minister of reconciliation (2 Corinthians 5:17-20), God's workmanship (Ephesians 2:10), the temple of the Holy Spirit (1 Corinthians 6:19), a disciple of Christ (John 13:15), a member of God's household (Ephesians 2:19) and a new creation (2 Corinthians 5:17) our past no longer shames us, controls us, labels us or defines us. These things, just like our personal I.D. that the Government gives us, identify us now. This is our new identity in Christ. As a result, we really are free to be who we were created to be (reflections of God, Himself [Colossians 3:12-14]) and to live for the purpose we were created for (to glorify God, worship God and make Him known [Romans 11:36]).

The reason it is so important to know what our identity is now that we are in Christ is not just because it changes us. It also changes how we treat others who are children of God. Imagine how we might respond to others, treat people, talk to them if we considered that they are or might be one of God's delights (Zechariah 2:8), the bride of Christ, a special and chosen instrument. Would it cause us to stop and ask would God treat me this way, "Would God treat the apple of His eye (Psalm 17:8), one of His excellent ones (Psalm 16:3) in such a way?" Because our identity comes through the grace and love of God, at the expense of Christ. In spite of whether we are deserving or not (we never can be) it shows us that He loved us first (1 John 4:9). As a result, it creates within us a desire to live with a heart of gratitude for our new identity. We, in turn, can be nobodies for Christ ministering to others the love and grace of Christ. As long as we try to build upon our identity through our efforts we will never enjoy being God's treasure. We will always be hoping we can do enough to be considered worthy of being loved by God. We also will likely not be instruments of grace but demanding, finger pointing, accusing Pharisees.

Not one of us will ever be truly faithful enough or obedient enough to merit the identity we have in Christ. This is why Paul says in Philippians 3:9, "I could not make myself acceptable to God by obeying the Law of Moses. God accepted me simply because of my faith in Christ." Faith in what? Faith that, because we have accepted Christ's sacrificial payment and have believed on Him who died for us, there is no longer any condemnation for those who are in Christ (Romans 8:1). This should then compel us to offer our lives as living sacrifices out of love and worship for the One who gave all. We do not do so to make the identity or ourselves more valuable, for our value does not come from us, but from the one who gave all (Titus 3:4-7).

Yet, when we choose to not live according to our new identity while our identity remains the same our relationship with God has been affected (Psalm 5:4, ESV). God is Holy and He cannot look upon sin (Habakkuk 1:13) and has utter distaste for sin. Sin is not something God takes lightly. Yet God does not treat us according to our sin but according to His grace, always (Psalms 103:10-14). Which is another aspect of our new identity and that when God sees us now He sees the perfect obedience of Christ and not our failed obedience (2 Corinthians 5:21). Not living accordingly to who we are now in Christ shows not only a lack of faithfulness, but also shows a lack of appreciation, a lack of understanding of who God is and what we have been given through Christ. It also removes the freedom we have in our new identity as we choose to return back to the cages that once controlled us. The reason our relationship becomes affected is that while God stands still with wide open loving arms we have chosen to remain in the cage of our old choices. In effect, we choose the confines of a cage, a lifestyle and its choices, that were contrary to what we were designed for. As we remain in this comfortable (because it's what we knew) cage, God stands outside waiting. God has not moved, we choose to be captives again in the cage (Isaiah 61:1). Thus whether the door is open or closed, we allow it to be a barrier between us and God.

We need to remember that part of our new identity is to be instruments (the mouth, hands and feet) of God's glory (His who He is, His character, His gifts) (Romans 6:13) and that is why the greatest reason we should choose to live accordingly is so that we reflect the love of an Almighty God, and allow Him to find deep pleasure in our worship of Him (Psalms 147:11) as we say thank you for making us yours. Yet, another aspect of our identity is we will never be as messed up as we were without Christ and as a result we know that if God loved us then, He will not love us less now if we fail to represent our new identity. Dr. Neil Anderson in his book *Victory Over the Darkness* shares, "The more you reaffirm who you are in Christ, the more your behavior will begin to reflect your true identity!" We would simply say, "**Amen!**"

What about obedience?

The war rages on, the papers, blogs, e-newsletters, read. The newscasts were filled with the daily happenings of the most current state of affairs, and in today's world that is bound to include one or two wars somewhere. Yet, there is a war that rages on. We guarantee that you will not hear about in most papers, blogs, e-newsletters or newscasts; unless it is specifically devoted to this topic. That is the news, that there is a war raging inside each individual child of God. Not only does it rage inside of us, but we have both unnamed and named assailants firing at us as we walk through each day; which in turn just makes some days hotter.

Yet, this is not a flesh and blood war but a war against forces that we cannot see. This is the battle Paul spoke of in Ephesians 6:12, "We are not fighting against humans. We are fighting against forces and authorities, and against rulers of darkness, and powers in the spiritual world." Every day we must make a choice (Romans 6:12-13) to serve our old master or serve one who calls us the apple of His eye, the excellent ones, the deeply desired ones, the ones He is passionate about, His chosen children, His instruments of grace, and the specific people chosen to be His royal priests. 1 Peter 1:9 says, "But you are God's chosen and special people. You are a group of royal priests and a holy nation. God has brought you out of darkness into His marvelous light. Now you must tell all the wonderful things that He has done. The Scriptures say." Make no mistake about it we are in a battle and we will fail more than we get it right. The reason we will fail is because our emotional ear and our mind can still hear and remember the voices of our old life screaming.

"Did you forget how much fun we used to have?" "You no longer matter." "You can handle it, you got it, you need no-one." And a host of other statements Satan and his little band of gloomy angels will help echo, scream, hurl attacks with and just plain make it hard to hear the Holy Spirit's voice.

It will seem as though it is almost impossible to not listen to those voices and make choices not in obedience to God, but according to whatever voice is speaking the loudest to us. This is the struggle we see with Paul in Romans 7:14-24. This is why the choice we must make at any given moment is to remind ourselves of the grace and love of God. This is why Paul encouraged us to renew our minds (Romans 12:2) and to make our first choice to read the Bible, so that the Holy Spirit's voice, as He points us to both old and new truth (John 14:26), is always the loudest voice we hear.

Before we came to Christ we did not have such choices, now we do (Romans 6:15-19). Yet we do not make such choices, as some would say, in order to come into a relationship with God. That comes through one simple choice to take Christ at His word or not when He said, "It is finished." If the relationship given through grace was dependent on our ability to do so it would not be grace (Romans 11:6).

Obedience that is motivated by anything other than we were loved first (1 John 4:9), and gratitude for the gift of salvation that comes through faith, is legalistic and wrong (Hebrews 11:6). Such motivation makes the work of Christ for us less than it actually is. The work of Christ was sufficient in and of itself (Romans 5:1-2). There is nothing more to do or that needs to be done (Romans 5:18-21). His work satisfied God's need for justice, that our failure to live in a way to please God brought (Romans 5:9). In fact, not only did we fail, we did not even recognize we were not living in a way pleasing to God and we were in fact enemies (Romans 5:10) and hostile towards God (Colossians 1:21, ESV). So Christ died for us, not because we were good, or could make ourselves respectable to God, but because we could not (Romans 5:6-8). So to say that now more must be done, or that there is need for us to do more is not making it about Jesus and as a result it really amounts to nothing at all done to bring us closer to God.

If such works were not needed before we came to Christ, they are not needed after. For God needs nothing from us (Acts 17:24-28). We came into the relationship through the grace of God offered freely to us through Christ, and we continue for-

ward in this relationship freely under the power and strength
of the Holy Spirit working through us (Galatians 3:1-4, Colossians 1:11). To say that we must do something that amounts
to keeping God happy is nothing more than our arrogance, and
our narcissistic nature that continues to make us think we need
to be approved of, or constantly taken notice of. Such arrogance
keeps us from not only resting totally in the Blood of Christ for
our salvation, but it also keeps us from believing and accepting
that there is nothing left to do, **really**, after we come to Christ!
So does that mean we should not be obedient, or choose to not
give sin power in our lives, **No**. Nor does it mean we should not
choose to recognize the old way of thinking or living, or acting
as dead to us now.

What it does mean, is that we do not have to make choices
that reflect our obedience to God, in order to keep, or get God's
favor. When we do make such choices we should not only always ask why we need to make such a choice, but what is our
motivation for making such choices. This is what Paul meant
when he knew his readers would ask the same questions after
finishing reading his letter at the end of chapter 5 in Romans
and he begins the next part of the letter with "Heaven Forbid"
(Romans 6:1)! The Bible is very clear that we are to recognize
our old ways as dead and to make choices that reflect that we
are now in a relationship with God (Colossians 3). Paul compares the way we used to live to the way we should live in Christ
in order to specifically show that we were once the servants of
Satan (Ephesians 2:2), but now we should look at ourselves as
servants of God (Romans 6:11-23). Christ said that those who
love Him, keep His commandments, and that the purpose of the
Holy Spirit is to remind us of those commandments and to keep
peace in our hearts when we fail (John 14:23-31).

So why be obedient now? Why choose to do things that
just seem utterly impossible at times? Truth is without the Holy
Spirit they are! Why do anything at all? Because we have been
freed to be able to do so (Galatians 5:1). The cages have been
destroyed, the doors have been opened and we have been set free

(Isaiah 61:1). We have been set free to be able to be what God intended us to be; that begins with the worship of Him and the obedience that comes out of that worship. We do not obey to get His love, but because we have it we can now obey Him out of love (1 John 5:2-3). Through our obedience we tell others who we allow to have the ultimate say in our lives and as a result prove our faithfulness (1 John 2:3-6) and we make Him known (1 Peter 2:12).

Timothy Keller says this about our motivation and for why we obey.

> God did not give the children of Israel the law (the Ten Commandments) and then have them say 'we'll do everything the Lord says' and then He says 'good, now I'll save you, I'll take you out of Egypt on eagle's wings, Rather, God saved them first. "Now, because I've saved you ... obey me.

That is why we should obey because God saved us first, still saves us first, and will save us first regardless of any response that comes from us; He has promised to finish what He started (Philippians 1:6). Paul said that it was Christ's love that was the reason for why he was obedient in 2 Corinthians 5:14, "For Christ's love compels us, because we are convinced that one died for all, and therefore all died." So each moment the first choice we must make is not to tighten our shoelaces in order to get ready to go or do it in our own strength or our own abilities, but to accept that we cannot. We cannot live in a way that pleases God without the grace that He so freely gives us. The second choice is to every day choose whether to serve the one who demanded our service or the One who now loves us in spite of whether we respond in kind.

To choose to make choices that reveal that we once were God's enemies, is to be enslaved again. The only choices that represent the freedom God has now given us are choices that reflect that we are indeed thankful that God has taken us off the hamster wheel, and allows us now the freedom to say thank you for loving me even when I could not even truly love myself. Then to offer our bodies as a living conduit, in which Christ lives through us, to point others to God's glory and the cross. Should we be obedient? **Yes!** In fact, now more so than ever, because of the grace freely given! The price was expensive and it was paid through the blood of the perfect lamb and it is really is now the least we can do (Romans 12:1).

Something bad is happening or has happened in my life. Is God punishing me?

One thing we can absolutely assure you: God is not punishing you or rewarding you for anything you may or may not do. Now, whether you bear some guilt for something you did — that is another question.

Often we do many stupid things which bring harm or discomfort or displeasure to ourselves and others. Even when we know that what is happening in our lives is a result of something we have done, we often express anger towards God because He did not save us from ourselves. Unfortunately, many people believe God needs some type of payment from us for His grace. Or they want to make sure we do not abuse God's gift of grace, so they tell us God is punishing us for some past misdeed.

Many who say this are taking Hebrews 12:6 out of context. "The Lord corrects the people he loves and disciplines those he calls his own." The type of discipline the Bible is referring to here is not like a parent to a mischievous child, but the focus of an athlete who prepares his body to run a race.

The work of making us what we were created to be is 100% God's! We have no part of it, nor will we ever have any part of it. While God may indeed stretch us out of our comfort zones and bring us to the point where it seems our peaceful existence has been totally disrupted, He does this not for or because of us, but for His glory (Isaiah 48:10).

When we conclude that a difficulty or tragedy is God punishing us, we have just made God's salvation **our** work and dependent on **our** perfect ability to live as He would have us live. When we were totally rebelling against God, He did not respond harshly, but rather according to His great love. So why would He respond differently now? Always remember God is far more interested in our character becoming Christ-like, than He is in us not suffering.

God will also not settle for playing second fiddle to anyone or anything. So whatever needs to be done to develop our character or make sure He is first, God will do. Remember: life's interruptions are designed by the Creator in order to bring us closer to His created purpose for us, which was to be in fellowship, praise Him and be individuals who reflect His character.

Suffering always comes with a purpose. If we consider suffering as coming from God, we discover that God is awakening in us a deeper understanding and knowledge of how much we are loved by **Him**. That love is exhibited by doing those things that we may not like or cause us to being angry at Him, but they also bring us closer to why we exist.

The answer to dealing with the suffering is not to look for a way to escape or remove the pain, but instead, actively seek the love of the Father, who gives us the strength to endure what we need in our most difficult times. That strength will also give us real hope to get through those times. God said, "My grace is sufficient for you, for my power is made perfect in weakness" (2 Corinthians 12:9).

Without those dark valleys, those times when it feels life has taken a baseball bat to our middle, we may never fully experience the love of the Father who provides His love during those times of lost hope. The comfort of knowing Jesus is never fully realized until your life is turned upside down. For, just as a tree whose roots are deepened during times of stress, so our lives are deepened during the most difficult times of life.

We can also rest assured that He has promised that all things will work to our best. As to what is best for us, it is for our best to be conformed to His image. Keeping that in mind, when suffering comes, allow yourselves and others to experience it in full, otherwise you may be hindering character development.

> God is calling us to live for the sake of Christ and to do that through suffering. Christ chose suffering; it didn't just happen to Him. He chose it as the way to create and perfect the church. Now He calls us to choose suffering. That is, He calls us to take up our cross and follow Him on the Calvary road and deny ourselves

and make sacrifices for the sake of ministering to the church and presenting His sufferings to the world.*

---

*   John Piper, *Desiring God: Meditations of a Christian Hedonist.* The Doubleday Religious Publishing Group. 2011, p 286.

Will reading my Bible and praying help me grow in grace?

The answer one might expect is that it can't hurt or Yes! In truth, without proper clarification both of these answers could be wrong. Seems hard to believe that reading the Bible and praying will not help you grow in grace or that reading the Bible or praying could hurt.

First, we need to understand the reason why that might be true in order to determine a proper answer to the question. Contrary to popular opinion, only those who have placed their faith in Christ for their eternal security can pray to God the Father (John 9:31), which says, "We know that God listens only to people who love and obey him. God doesn't listen to sinners." Proverbs 15:29 also says, "The Lord never even hears the prayers of the wicked, but he answers the prayers of all who obey him. Prayer is a gift for those who have become God's children."

Prayer is also not about us bringing a wish list to God. Such thinking shows a lack of understanding of who God is. When Christ said "If you ask anything in my name" He was not opening Trinity Inc.'s company checkbook so He could cover the operating expenses of allowing us to live it up to our heart's desire. Instead, Jesus was telling those listening that God eagerly waits to grant those prayer requests that honor **Him!**

What desires honor God? Again, contrary to popular opinion, those desires have little to do with the comfort and peacefulness of our life, wealth, health or happiness. They do have everything to do with becoming or returning back to our original created purpose, which was to praise Him for being God and to be His mouthpieces, arms, and hands of generosity, goodness, mercy, and grace by serving others.

Any prayer that does not come from a heart of faith and knowledge that we are now the chosen bride of Christ is sin (Romans 14:23). When our hearts have been shaped with an understanding and acceptance of that faith, we will develop hearts which seek to worship, glorify and honor the Father, seek the

Father's will in our lives, and reflect a desire to be instruments of His glory and to be vessels to be used to build His kingdom. Those hearts will pray in ways that honor the Father and bring requests the Father eagerly awaits to answer.

So praying in any other way may indeed be harmful. An obstinate heart, self-centered heart treats God like He is there to grant our every wish.

When it comes to reading our Bible, there are also ways in which it can be harmful. If we are just picking verses out of the Bible and trying to apply them to our lives, this could indeed be harmful. Imagine someone asking themselves what God wants them to do at the moment. So they open their Bible and it falls to Matthew 27:5 which is where Judas went out and hanged himself. "OK God, if that's what you want!" Now that seems absurd. No one would really do that, right? However, while many may not go to such drastic extremes, many do not put the time and study into the Word of God in order to read and understand passages in the context they are written. So they take passages out of context and use them improperly.

This is a common occurrence that causes much harm spirituality to individuals and to Christ's Church all the time. The need for proper handling of God's Word cannot be overstated. Paul said in 2 Timothy 2:15, "Do your best to win God's approval as a worker who doesn't need to be ashamed and who teaches only the true message." "What God has said isn't only alive and active! It is sharper than any double-edged sword" (Hebrews 4:12).

Imagine taking a sharp, double-edged sword with people standing around and handling it carelessly. There would be a real good chance that someone might get hurt. The same can be said for the handling of God's Word. When handled incorrectly, someone may indeed get hurt, including yourself. This is why it is imperative to be in a good Bible teaching church, as well as listening to and reading those who have walked on this journey longer than us.

As you trust the Holy Spirit, He will help you discern truth and show you how to hold fast to that which is good (1Thessalonians 5:21). Keep this in mind, the Bible is not a book to be devoured or a novel to be conquered, it is the inspired Word of God to be ingested, chewed on and then applied.

Many try to read through the Bible in one calendar year. But if we read it in such a way as to understand and commit principles to memory, it may be a more reasonable goal to do it in three to five years. We must also be careful of reading into God's Word what we **want** to see. When we are looking for an answer or direction from God, look at passages in context with the complete story. The Holy Spirit will always speak to us through the Word of God but it must always be read with the whole book in mind and not just a single verse or passage alone. Errors in trying to determine what a certain passage may be saying lead to errors in application. The other thing to keep in mind is that God's Word is not written to us but about God and our story in light of Who God is.

There is one more aspect we must consider. Our being made what we were designed to be is a complete work of God, through the Holy Spirit. Reading the Bible or praying will not add one bit of spiritual growth, change or development apart from the Work of The Holy Spirit. Imagine being married and never spending time talking or listening to your spouse. You really would not have much of a relationship, would you? So the same is true with God. As we pray we are communicating with Him, and as we read His Word through the power of the Holy Spirit, God communicates with us, revealing who He is, how much He loves us and who we are. Such wonderful truths will always result in a life that reveals that life to others. Which is the purpose of reading the Bible and prayer.

How do I read my Bible?

There seems to be countless Bible reading plans, books on the best ways to read the Bible and thousands of devotionals to guide us through such an endeavor. The first thing we would say is that the Bible is not a book to be quickly devoured, a novel to be placed lightly by the bedside table, nor is it a self- help book to which we run to find the nearest answer to solve our ongoing dilemmas or today's pressing problem(s).

The second thing we would state is that it makes little sense **to read the Bible without Christ or someone who does know Christ as their Savior.** You might as well pick up the latest scribbled notes of a foreign language you want to learn. In fact, if you are looking for something to read, do that as it will indeed appear to make more sense.

Do not read the Bible with the purpose of finding personal instruction or self-help because it's a popular book. Do not pull single and random passages out of it to find answers, meaning and direction in your life. **The Bible is the greatest story ever written, yet it really is not our story.** It is the story of how the Creator of the Universe created us, knew we would fall in sin, and so He prepared a way before He created one thing in this world, to redeem us back to Himself.

It is the story of that plan through history and how, after we fell, we continued to seek our own way, desire our own way and **could do nothing that represents who God is.** Knowing that, the story shows how He continues to chase us, how extravagantly He loves us, and His plan of action in order to one day present us to the praise and the glory of **His** name. Everything we read in God's Word should be read in that light and under that microscope.

The Bible really does consist of perfect law countered by merciful grace. As God's laws leave no doubt about how condemned we are, our need for change and what living a life in obedience to God looks like, His love is shown not only through grace but also through His perfect law.

For God truly does love and care about us and wants what is best for us, and it is through the law He reveals His goodness to us. Grace, though costly to God, is given freely to us so that we might be able to live the law of God.

Grace is the Miracle-Gro® upon which the seed of grace is given birth and grows to maturity. The law shows us how far we need to travel and grace enables us to get there.

This is the Bible, the Word of God, and when approached with this perspective, the chances of error of interpretation and application always diminishes. The Bible is also the inerrant, life-breathed Word of God as written by the original authors through the inspiration of His Spirit. Because it is the life-breathed Word of God, the Holy Spirit works through the Bible as we read or listen, to sanctify us and enable us one day to be presented as the masterpiece of God (2 Timothy 3:16). If the greatest thing is "faith expressed through love" (Galatians 5:6), and "faith comes by hearing" (Romans 10:17) or listening to Jesus' Word, then it only makes sense that hearing and reading God's Word is the key to growing in love for our Father and for others.

Understanding all of these things help us to understand why reading the Bible through in a year may not be possible. As we read it with a heart and a desire to digest it, we come to a deeper understanding of God's story and what He has to say to us as individuals through that story. Working to read it through a three to five year plan may indeed be more feasible.

Reading it systematically may help us to read with a purpose as long as the system keeps the above truths in mind. Yet, we are free to read it whenever and however we like, as far as position, time and place.

Reading the Bible with the intent of having daily devotions that bring some form of pickup or uplift for the day may or may not take away our dependence on God. This is because instead of reliance upon God, it becomes about our personal disciplines. We really are free to worship the One who calls us **His** beloved and there is no greater way to reflect this than how we approach **His** Word.

Life gets in the way sometimes and, suddenly before we realize it, we have missed a day, two or three or even more. Remember, **there really is no condemnation to those who are in Christ Jesus.** When you are ready, take a minute and confess your failure to keep God your #1 priority and you will find Him waiting! He really does want us to approach Him in faith and with a cheerful heart. For when we take time to study God's Word, we are giving of ourselves.

No, this is not encouraging flippancy, carelessness or a lack of reverence, but quite the opposite. **For anything we do, which is not done based on faith motivation, is sin** (Hebrews 11:6). Faith motivation is based on a heart of gratitude towards God for providing a way to escape an eternal destiny filled with abandoned hope.

As we read God's Word, we discover God's law, which shows us how we were created to be and live. As grace creates the changes that the law points out, they are reflected in our desires, actions and thoughts. One of the primary changes it will create is the desire to share God's Word with others.

In order to do that effectively, we will need to become **students and craftsmen of God's Word**, thus enabling us to have an answer for every man that asks of us the reason why we believe what we believe. That is why it is best to study God's Word with good tools.

Just as any craftsman in any field has tools that enable him to perform his craft, so does a student or craftsman of God's Word. Tools like a good concordance, a Bible dictionary, a commentary and encyclopedia will go a long way in enabling us to have those answers.

Often we will come across a passage that is difficult to understand. Always keep in mind that the Bible is sufficient in and of itself, interprets itself and that the Holy Spirit will help you come to a deeper understanding through other parts of God's Word that may be easier to understand. We will always be safe when before interpretation and application we remember God never contradicts Himself and neither does His Word.

Keep in mind, **the Word of God is a two edged sword**, a sharp one at that (Hebrews 4:12). Be careful when waving it around in other people faces, you really could put someone's eye out with it. Serious injuries have occurred because it was not handled carefully, that's why it comes with its own God General Warning.

Have you ever had someone read an article, tell you about the article, and then as you sat down to read it you thought, "Where and how did they get **that** out of this article?" We all do it and when we do, it is called placing our own inference or built in bias into what we read. When studying the Bible, be careful of pre-conceived thinking, bias or prejudice. Read with an open mind to what the Holy Spirit wants to reveal to us and you will find God's principles become more clear, personal behavior getting closer to Christ's and your life more inspired to live for the One who gave all. The Holy Spirit's chief job is to make Christ known and to always redirect your focus on Jesus. You will find the true purpose of God's Word is not a subject to be mastered, but a life to be studied. As you study the life of the perfect Lamb that was slain, you will find your life taking on the likeness of His life.

There are those times when we come to have **an intentional time of meeting with God**. We come with our heart desiring a more intimate relationship with our Father, as we pray and read **His** Word. These times will be as original as we are and should be done with variety and the spice of creativity. If having a plan, a scheduled time helps with that intentionality then do so with a heart that chooses this in freedom, not compulsion.

There are many ways to approach God's Word. The ways do not matter as much as does understanding that one of the greatest ways God tells us how crazy **He** is about us is through His Word. It is always fresh as it renews us daily. The Holy Spirit works like a waterfall flowing over us as we meditate on those precious words. It is through God's inspired words we discover who we are, who Jesus is, and in doing so, who we were meant to be.

Let it never be forgotten that, although we may do nothing about the Word we hear, the Word will do something to us. The same sun melts ice and hardens clay, and the Word of God humbles or hardens the human heart. Truth heard and not acted upon is a dangerous thing. Spiritual impulses which are not translated into action have a disastrous reaction.[*]

---

[*] Vance Havner, *Jesus Only*. F.H. Revell Company. 1969, Chapter 11.

How do I pray?

Many times when someone asks "How should I pray" somebody will direct them to Jesus' prayer in Matthew 6:9-13 where He said, "You should pray like this: ..." While He did give this as an example, implying that this is the only way to pray gives a very narrow focus and pulls a passage out of scripture and away from the whole Bible. When this happens we end up with a disconnected, disjointed view of not only that passage but all of God's Word. Along with an answer that is incorrect. Jesus' prayer is merely an outline of how we are to approach God and contains some of the main things we should pray about.

There are many examples of Christ praying in various ways. In Luke 18:9-14, Jesus points to the difference between a sinner's prayer and the prayer of a Pharisee. He says that the sinner's prayer will be heard.

Both prayer and grace are gifts from God and because of Jesus, we are able to appear before God in prayer and not by something we have been able to muster on our own. Prayer is a free gift given to believers.

We should come to God in prayer with a heart of gratitude and humility, recognizing that He indeed is God and we are not. And yet, even here none of us are perfect. We all continue to seek our own interests and try to impress God with our most recent performances as we say, "Hey God, did you see what I did there?" while God replies "Yep, sorry the reason you did that was to impress me, gain my favor, and keep my favor. It's not necessary because you missed the point. It isn't about me noticing you, but you remembering I'm God, Creator and Giver. I really don't need or require or desire anything from you."

We also will have times that we question, scream, holler, and exclaim, "What are You doing?" Never be afraid to admit your feelings to God, even anger and frustration. When we look at the Old Testament we see the prophets expressing their anger to God, Jonah 4:1-5, their desire to die and be left alone, 1 Kings 19:1-10, and their questioning of God, Job 10:1-7. Even

Christ questioned and cried out to God in agony, Luke 22:41-46. The next requirement in prayer is **honesty!** Remember God is all-knowing so we might as well name it and claim it! Let **Him** know the raw honesty which comes when life has hit you upside the head with a two by four and left you feeling dazed and confused. Many people are closet complainers, hidden rationalizers as they reason in their minds that it is okay to not be human and not acknowledge those raw feelings. So they hide in closets, as a manner of speech, trying to repress or keep down what is humanly impossible to grasp.

God expects us to get angry and discouraged, cry out with questions and even shout. He knows that life can wear us out and get us down and that the drudgery and pain of everyday life can be wearisome, over-burdening and extremely difficult for us. He knows we are human, after all He created us and as a result has compassion on us. Read Psalm 103:10-14.

In speaking of honesty, remember that in grace we can come freely, but unconfessed sin can hinder our time spent in prayer, in the ability to listen and to hear the Father. Because of grace, the Father eagerly awaits as we change our mind about what we are doing wrong, confess it and accept the forgiveness that stands waiting for us. This is also part of being humble and remembering that He chose us, we did not choose **Him**.

It is an error to teach that sin keeps us from coming to God or that God will not hear us. While the sin that hinders our faculties from doing anything Godward does hinder our prayer, **God always hears the prayers of those who have accepted Christ as their Savior.** There is not one of us who is not without sin, who does not continue in sin, even if that sin is merely the sin of self-sufficiency. There is never a moment of time we are not without sin. So relax, it's okay, **He** said it, so there is something else you can name and claim — our inability to be without sin!

Do not be misled in thinking that you must confess **every** sin **before** we come to prayer as that is partly an error. The truth is we can never fully confess all of our sins enough to deserve, earn or receive the right to come to God. We do not come to the

Father because of something we have done but because of what Christ accomplished. The Father does not hear our prayers because we have made ourselves righteous in His eyes, but because Christ has paid the price for us to do so. **Now Jesus serves as our mediator, our intercessor before the Father** (Romans 8:34).

In fact **our very words must be translated by the Holy Spirit as we pray** (Romans 8:26). In this we find the importance of confession, humility and acknowledgment that He is God. That importance being us bending our mind's knee to the Father and accepting who He is and who we are not. Our confession of our sins, our acknowledgment that God is God and we are not, is for us, not for God.

The next guideline about how we should pray is a prayer should always be intentional. "Come now and let us reason together" (Isaiah 1:18). God is inviting us to come and talk it over. Remember God is our loving, caring Father and He really does want to sit down with us to share and talk, just as we might with a friend or our earthly father.

The best times of prayer are when we sit down to meet with God for a specific purpose. Such times will bring extraordinary blessings as we come in humility, gratefulness and honesty, even brokenness and deep sharing, which may possibly bring deep healing of wounds we all suffer as we live on this planet.

Remember, prayer is a two-way conversation, so listen to the Holy Spirit's promptings, that tender, quiet inner voice that brings a verse to mind or something someone said that causes us to reflect on the wonder and character of God while we are praying. It is these times of listening prayer that push us into a deeper relationship.

We should always keep in mind the importance of seeking to measure all things we may hear to God's inspired Word to see that it stacks up and holds up against the source of all ultimate truth, even if what we heard appears to be a good thought or word. We do not take what we thought or heard with our emotional ears and use it as a complement to God's Word, but rather we take God's Word to determine if what we think we heard is accurate.

Sitting, standing, laying prostrate, eyes open, eyes closed, alone or with a crowd, matters not at all, as we really are free. In fact, we are free to **not** communicate with God at all. Yet the purpose of prayer is to build our relationship with the One who calls us, **His** Beloved.

A heart of gratitude comes from recognizing that the Wicked Witch of OZ fame (you know, the one that Dorothy's house landed on!) looks better than we do, and yet God still loved us enough to give us a free gift. It is the receipt of that gift which should create within us a desire not just to communicate with God but also to have a relationship with Him which always comes through an intimate two-way conversation with anyone, especially God.

So what is the proper way to pray? Philippians 4:6-7 echoes everything we have already listed, stating that we should pray with a grateful, humble, honest, intentional heart expressing all thoughts, burdens, cares, hurts, offenses, needs and desires. God really does eagerly await to answer those prayers of our desires that make the most of **Him**, eagerly and aggressively.

If we follow the message of Philippians 2:1-4, our prayers will be filled not only with our purposes, but also the purposes of others. As we grow in our love of the Father and others, we truly will find our greatest pleasure in bringing the cares of others to Him.

Prayer is indeed the ultimate privilege of the believer. It is the deepest blessing in being able to have a relationship with God and to find our enjoyment in worshiping **Him**. Because it is a deeply intentional part of our relationship, there is no secret formula or right or wrong way, thus it is the freedom we are now given.

We may find the way we pray is as distinct about us, as the very personality that makes us unique. Just as God did not create two people exactly the same, He rarely communicates with two people in exactly the same way. So experience it in it's entirety, seek a true relationship and enjoy the freedom that comes with the ability to have a truly unique two-way conversation with the Creator of the Universe.

> Prayer should not be regarded as a duty which must be performed, but rather as a privilege to be enjoyed, a rare delight that is always revealing some new beauty.*

---

*   E.M. Bounds, *Purpose of Prayer.* Whitaker House. 1997, Chapter 7

How does God use the Bible and prayer to communicate to me? Are there other ways God communicates to me?

There may indeed be other ways in which God may speak to us, but the Bible should always be the last word. Everything else is not complementary to God's Word but to be judged by God's Word. Often when someone says they have a "word" for us from God or we think we have heard something, God may have already said something about that very thing in His Word.

If God's Word is in agreement then we know that what we are being told or what we think we heard through the voice of our conscious or our emotional mind's ear, may indeed be of and from God. However, if it is unclear, or contradicts God's Word, then be careful for it may be from another source.

Paul said to **"hold true to that which is good"** (1 Thessalonians 5:21) and Peter said also **"that there exist many false teachings"** (2 Peter 2:1). Through our times in prayer we may hear the inner promptings through our emotional mind's ear of the Holy Spirit as a thought or a voice that glorifies, honors, calls us to worship or to offer our daily lives as an instrument of His glory.

That is indeed one way to ensure what we think we heard is of God. When something originates from Heaven and we offer it back to God, those are prayers God eagerly awaits with a response. Remember Satan has no desire to draw us away from our own desires and keep us focused totally on God.

Remember, there are no coincidences, no surprises with God, nor any stray molecules with **Him. He** really is in total control of every molecule (1 Samuel 2:6, 1 Chronicles 29:11-12, Job 12:23, Job 42:2, Psalms 115:3, Isaiah 46:9-10, Ecclesiastes 7:13-14, Isaiah 45:7, Daniel 2:21, Acts 17:24-28)! Those circumstantial events that appear in our lives, may be the very directional hand of God bringing events and people into our lives. There are no random happenings, circumstances, accidental timings, destiny, fate, for indeed God is in complete control and He arranges all such things appearing as such, God may use us to pray for, about or minister to them. So another way God speaks to us is through the circumstances of life.

Perhaps as we are praying or going through our day a name or a Bible verse may pop into our minds. A particular burden for someone or some circumstance may come pressing on us with extreme weight and care. This may be the prompting of the Holy Spirit to pray or lift a certain person or situation up in prayer. A scripture verse that God needs to bring to our attention may be for us to meditate on, not necessarily act on, but praying it back to God is a good response. Then wait and see as time moves on how God reveals a significance to that verse.

The more time we spend in the Word of God, the more **the Holy Spirit will use God's Word to illuminate God's truth** to us by bringing verses to mind in certain situations. As you grow in your relationship with God, your maturity of understanding will increase your ability to rightly use **His** Word. **He** may bring verses to mind as you are speaking with someone else about Him. Through that God will be using you to speak into the lives of others and He will also use others to speak into your life. However, do not just randomly take such verses, but go seek the truth, study them in context with the whole of God's Word. Remember, if there is truth, God will reveal it.

We can rest assured that Satan will rarely ignite in us a passion for building God's Kingdom. That would be quite foolish on his part, would it not? Let's keep in mind, a **passion** is not the same thing as seeing a need or feeling like contributing towards something or getting casually involved in something. A passion is that thing that burns so strong, so brightly, so fervently in us that it consumes us till we do something about it. Satan may very well show us many needs, things we can do and be involved in as he waters down that one single-minded purpose or focus which creates within us a burning passion to do something within God's Kingdom.

It is this Godly passion that leads to a Kingdom ambition which is sparked by the Holy Spirit that God may use to show us a special purpose or plan He has for us. There never arises doubt or a lack of certainty when a need, passion, or purpose is sparked by God in us to do something.

Yes, there are many ways in which the Spirit of God may communicate to us if we are listening. We will find ourselves listening more as we grow in our relationship with our Beloved. However, no matter what way He communicates with us, all these ways should always be defined as communication from God by **His** Word. **So get to know the Father, who calls you His beloved and chosen bride, better.**

> Real prayer is communion with God, so that there will be common thoughts between His mind and ours. What is needed is for Him to fill our hearts with His thoughts, and then His desires will become our desires flowing back to Him.*

---

* Arthur W. Pink, *Sovereignty of God.* Wilder Publications. 2009, p 216

Will God give me more than I can handle?

A common saying that is often uttered when someone is going through a time of suffering is "God will not give us more than we can handle." To which someone hearing this statement will either say out loud or think "Does God think I'm superman?" If you have had someone say this to you please feel free to laugh, otherwise you may do something you will regret later. If you never have had someone say this to you then consider yourself extremely blessed.

Such a statement comes from well meaning friends or people we know, like the ones we find in the book or the story of Job. We know these kinds of friends. They are the ones that no matter how much life is burning down on us at the moment, always seem to have an analogy or a piece of unfettered, unasked for advice. Such words rarely have the effect of making us feel more encouraged. We feel that there is indeed something terribly wrong with us, that we must be complete failures and are totally missing the boat. Not just missing the boat once, but it came again and we still missed it. "If we only had more faith," we think! Job's friends made him feel this way and are the best example given in the Bible of why the best kind of friends during times of suffering are often those whose voices are quiet. That is why such words are often more torture, or add to the suffering rather then easing it. As they may bring guilt, feelings of hopelessness, and deeper despair, which will always bring more pain in a time of where there is already so much pain.

There is another effect that comes through advice like this. It may cause us to hide, as we bury our pain in activity. We may end up holding and keeping our pain in. We may even try to pretend that what we are feeling is not real. We falsely believe that we can handle it ourselves, needing no one. We will often find ourselves uttering such words or thinking such words as "I can handle it!" or "I can do this!" These feelings, the hiding, ignoring, burying ultimately come from one of two issues. The first being pride, a pride that says "I got this." The second being idolization (whatever it is that we place in our lives to bring us feelings of comfort or ease or happiness), where we end up putting something (always smaller) in a place that only God can fulfill. Both of these will keep us from being strengthened and empowered (Colossians 1:11) by God's grace to move past such difficult times in our lives. We need to always remember that needing no one will always mean God. And these types of sentiments and attitudes will always keep us from coming to prayer and drawing upon God to walk through such dark times. As a result it may either seem like they last longer than they should, or never go away.

So where does such a quote come from, here's a hint: **Not the Bible!** Often 1 Corinthians 10:13 is the verse used to tell this to others. Here is the verse often referred to, "You are tempted in the same way that everyone else is tempted. But God can be trusted not to let you be tempted too much, and he will show you how to escape from your temptations." Notice Paul is speaking about temptations here and not suffering. There is a big difference between suffering and temptations. Suffering may or may not be something that is a consequence of our own choices and actions. Our choice to yield to temptation or not is always our choice. The temptation in suffering is not the suffering, but how we choose to handle it. In other words, what are the choices we are making as a result of the suffering?

Do we choose to hide it, handle it on our own, turn to something other than God, allow something smaller than God to bring us comfort and relief, or do we humble ourselves and admit that we are absolutely incapable of handling this; pleading to God for delivery and the grace to get through. Often, it is this very decision we must make each time we encounter suffering, for the very reason is why we may be encountering suffering.

Because of His great love towards us, God will do whatever He needs to do to bring us to the point in which we come out of our comfort zones and begin to make a choice of not relying on our strength, but asking Him for the grace and strength to get through it. It is always God's purpose in our sanctifying process to change us, stretch us, and push us beyond our boundaries and/or quite possibly, mess up a peaceful, easy life. God wants to become preeminent in our lives. When we feel we have no answers and no strength left, we will find our strength in Him. What Paul is saying in 1 Corinthians 10:13 is that every time life hits us with a baseball bat, God, through His grace, will empower us to make choices reflecting that He is indeed our strength. Yet it is a choice that we must make every time that it seems like everything is coming apart at the seams. Remember, it is not the suffering, but how we respond to it that is the temptation. Even if it seems, at times, it will break us in two. In effect, that is His purpose, to bring us to the point where He breaks us of the strength in ourselves. It is when we are weak that He is strong and most glorified (2 Corinthians 12:9).

This is the decision we see Christ making in the garden and a perfect example of making the right choice even when all Hell is literally coming against Him. In Matthew 26:39 we see Christ right before He is getting ready to walk the Calvary Road (the journey that would lead Him to the cross). "My Father, if it is possible, don't make me suffer by having me drink from this cup. But do what You want, and not what I want." Christ set the standard of how to cry out when life just seems like it is piling on just one unbearable incident after another.

We see the reason for why we suffer or why God allows or designs suffering in our lives through the words of Paul in 2 Corinthians 1:8-10. Paul utters that not only what they were suffering was beyond what they could bear but they wanted to die. Then he tells us why they were allowed to go through such dark times in verse nine, "this made us stop trusting in ourselves and start trusting God, who raises the dead to life." Catch that last part: it is a comparison. Sure, we can trust in our own strength, but when was the last time you or someone you knew raised someone from the dead?

So, that really is the ultimate decision in those times when the heat of life is not just giving you a suntan but giving you third degree burns. It is a decision to choose to remain prideful and think we can handle it on our own, or turn to something smaller than God, or we can grab hold of resurrection power through God's freely given grace. This is why Peter calls on us to offer it all up, lay it all down, leave it all with God (1 Peter 1:5-7). The whole point of the Christian life, whether it be relying on God to make us like Christ, or to enable us to give Him our obedience; our worship; to live our lives for others is to learn that it is not done through our strength. Nor through putting up facades that keep others from seeing that we are failing, but to humble ourselves so that we can receive the grace God wants to lavish on us. So that we can be obedient, worship God, and serve others.

One of the ways God helps us to endure such times is through the fellowship and comfort of our brothers and sisters in Christ. As we come alongside those who are suffering or allow others to come along side us, we may realize that not only has the burden gotten lighter, but it seems like Jesus Himself is closer. Provided that the ones we are getting close to, or we ourselves, are not bringing words that tells others how they, or we are failing. Rather, we are bringing words that tell how an Almighty God loves us when we ourselves did not know we needed such love or deserved such love (Galatians 6:1-3).

As the truth of the gospel (God loves us even at our worst and made a way for us to come back into a relationship with Him) becomes more real to us, it will become easier to make these type of choices. Choices that come from a heart of not only gratitude (Psalms 100:2) that reveal the love of God to others even in times of deep stress, keeping a tight handle on something, seeking comfort from something smaller than God or trying to handle it on our own, reveal a lack of understanding of that love and the power of grace that God wants to lavish on each of us in abundance, especially during times of deep stress.

> Suffering itself does not rob you of joy — idolatry does. If you're suffering and you're angry, bitter, and joyless it means you've idolized-and felt entitled to-whatever it is you're losing. Entitlement and self-

pity stem from our belief that we deserve more than what we're getting-love, attention, respect, approval. The gospel, however, frees us to revel in our expendability! The gospel alone provides us with the foundation to maintain radical joy in remarkable loss. Joylessness and bitterness in the crucible of pain happens when we lose something (or think we deserve something) that we've held onto more tightly than God.*

* Tchividjian, Tullian. (Blogpost) *The Gospel Coalition.* November 11, 2010, "Suffering Does Not Rob You Of Joy – Idolatry Does"

How do I get more of the Holy Spirit?

We do not **get** the Holy Spirit as in something we should acquire, as some teach. For the Holy Spirit is not an essence or an entity. He is a person just like the rest of the Trinity. We are told in scripture that the Holy Spirit is indeed God.

In the Acts of the apostles, Peter tells Ananias that Satan had filled his heart to lie to the Holy Spirit (Acts 5:3) and that he had not lied to man, but to God. Second Corinthians 13:14 says that not only do we worship the Father and Son but also the Holy Spirit. First Corinthians 2:10-11 attributes to the Holy Spirit the ability to know all things like God does. Because He is eternal (Hebrews 9:14) and referred to as God (1 Corinthians 6:19-20) we see He has the attributes, qualities and deity of God. This evidence proves beyond doubt that the Holy Spirit is the third member of the Trinity.

Because Christ identifies the Holy Spirit as a person like Himself, we have proof that the Holy Spirit has qualities of a person (John 14:26, 15:26, 16:7). Yet the Bible does not stop there, but goes on and lists qualities only a person can have:

- Thinks and knows (1 Corinthians 2:10).
- He can be grieved (Ephesians 4:30).
- He makes decisions according to His will (1 Corinthians 12:7-11).

We know that we do not get God, God gets us. Neither do we acquire or get more of God, so the same applies for the Holy Spirit. For indeed one does not get more of a person. All members of the Trinity are involved in the work of our salvation. The Holy Spirit plays the following roles in our salvation process and in our lives:

- He is the warranty of our heritage as children of God (Ephesians 1:13-14). It is the Holy Spirit that keeps us eternally secure in our relationship with God. Not anything we can or do.

- Through the Holy Spirit God's word has now become a living two-edged sword, as He illuminates all truth (John 16:13-14).
- The Holy Spirit enables us to live the way God wants us to and in the process to become more like we were designed to be (Romans 8:11).
- It is through the Holy Spirit that we gain the power to fight sin (Romans 8:5-6).
- Through His enabling us to fight sin, He changes us(1 Peter 1:2, 2 Thessalonians 2:13).
- He makes known the love of God in our hearts (Romans 5:5).
- The Holy Spirit is the one that works through us to glorify God and serve others (Philippians 2:16).
- He is the One who makes sure of our promised eternal life one day, that we will indeed join Christ in day to day existence with a new body, mind and spirit (2 Corinthians 1:21-22, Romans 8:30)!

Christ said, "You search the Scriptures, because you think you will find eternal life in them. The Scriptures tell about me" (John 5:39). He also said, "The Spirit will bring glory to me by taking my message and telling it to you" (John 16:14).

When we are being controlled by the Holy Spirit, our focus will indeed be on Jesus. That is the task, responsibility and function of the Holy Ghost. If our focus is only on or about what the Holy Spirit **does** and **His** gifts, what He can do for us or give us, and what we can **do** through Him, then our view and attitude about the Holy Spirit and **His** work may or may not be out of balance, wrong and not biblical. The Holy Spirit's job is not to highlight His own work but to always bring our attention to Christ and His finished work.

A strong indication that someone is speaking in Spirit and in truth occurs when the listener forgets the person speaking and only hears and sees Christ and the message of the Cross. So let us not seek, vote for, pursue or promote the "campaign manager," but rather the One who the campaign is about.

We have just spent time identifying who the Holy Spirit is, and what He does, now we need to finish answering the question of "How do we receive the Holy Spirit?"

If we believe Paul when he said in Ephesians 1:3, "Praise the God and Father of our Lord Jesus Christ for the spiritual blessings that Christ has brought us from heaven!" We can accept that the Holy Spirit is among those blessings and became a part of us the moment we believed in Jesus Christ for our salvation. Paul echoes this when he says in Romans 8:9, "You are no longer ruled by your desires, but by God's Spirit, who lives in you. People who don't have the Spirit of Christ in them don't belong to him."

As already mentioned, the Holy Spirit is the promise of our inheritance (eternal treasure, Ephesians 1:13-14). The Holy Spirit resides with us and in us assuring that the eternal life we have been promised with God, does indeed happen. As He continues to change us and prepare us to be in the presence of God for all eternity. So if the Holy Spirit did not come to reside within us, upon our belief in Jesus as our Savior, we indeed cannot be guaranteed eternal life. It never is about how we get more of the Holy Spirit, as in that we are to pursue Him. Neither does the Holy Spirit come upon us as we mature or become more obedient to God, as some may teach. We could never be obedient, repentant or deserving enough to get anything from God, much less God himself. **No!** The Holy Spirit freely takes up residence in us upon our commitment to Christ (1 Corinthians 6:19).

The Holy Spirit desires not to be pursued, chased, sought after. **His** only desire is to bring total focused attention to Jesus, who paid all debt and for whom one day every knee shall bow and every tongue shall confess (Philippians 2:10-11).

God, through the Holy Spirit, gives us our spiritual gifts and brings those gifts to visibility and full use as He changes us. This is **His** work and not ours, nor is it dependent on us.

As our desires grow to pray, read God's Word, and our ability to determine what the Bible says and how to apply it in our lives grows, other changes happen. We will seek to develop a relationship and share **His** Word with others. Our desires become those that honor God, our heart begins to know nothing other than God and His grace, and our passions develop to be an active part of building God's Kingdom. We can be sure the Holy Spirit is alive and well within us and actively at work.

As we walk on this journey of grace, it may appear that we are indeed exhibiting more of the gifts and fruits of God in our lives. This most assuredly comes as a result of our maturing through the sanctifying work of the Holy Spirit. The Holy Spirit is already completely with us, working in us and for us as He brings us closer to the created purpose that God the Father intended.

> To explain this a little further: Only the soul and the body are the natural constituent parts of men and women. The Spirit is not in the fundamental nature of humans but is the supernatural gift of God, to be found in Christians only.*

---

*   John Wesley, *How To Pray: The Best of John Wesley on Prayer.* Barbour Publishing, Inc. 2008.

Will I hear God speak to me?

There is a lot of confusion and discourse about this question and a lot of wrong answers as it pertains to this question. Often we will have someone say "God spoke to me" or "God gave me a word for you." Even worse someone will say to you "the reason God is not speaking to you is because you're disobedient."

> *Everything in the Scriptures is God's Word. All of it is useful for teaching and helping people and for correcting them and showing them how to live.* (2 Timothy 3:16)

The Bible tells us the story of God, the plan that was set in place before the creation of the world, who the plan is carried through and how it relates to us. As such, it has divine authority as to what God has said to mankind. It has the final authority in all matters of faith and practice. We need no other book to deliver God's message of faith; it really is sufficient and final. Saying that the Bible is clear does not say that everything written within it is perfectly clear but rather what God **needs** for us to know He has made known, leaving no doubt as to what God **intends** for us to know. If one passage is unclear another passage will help us to bring a clarity and an understanding to the first.

So all discussion of "God spoke to me" needs to come with the understanding of these basic tenets and truths. Everything else must be judged accordingly. Often the very thing someone is telling you that God told them, or the "word" they have for you, can already be found in the Word of God. This self-delivery statement is to bring glory to themselves, to make themselves appear important or significant or special. God does not give or share His glory with others. "My name is the Lord! I won't let idols or humans share my glory and praise" (Isaiah 42:8). Scripture also stresses the importance of "testing all things and holding true to that which is good" (1 Thessalonians 5:21). "... there are indeed many false prophets who will try to deceive you" (1 John 4:1).

We will encounter many along the way who will describe themselves as biblical teachers or claim to know God's Word, so it is important to study, so that we become craftsmen ourselves and can tell the difference between those who are genuine and those who are not. "Do your best to present yourself to God as one approved, a worker who has no need to be ashamed, rightly handling the word of truth" (2 Timothy 2:15).

What does it mean to be a part of God's family?

This is the reason for which we were created, to be a part of God's family. Unfortunately, due to the sin of one man (Adam), that family was broken. So instead of being naturally born into God's family, as some may teach, we were instead born cast off from God's family.

Romans 9:8 and Ephesians 2:3 say "that we are born as children of wrath." When we accept Christ as our Savior, we are welcomed into a global family and a heavenly body as God's children (John 1:12, Romans 8:16, 1 John 3:1-2). So now that you are part of God's family, we have brothers and sisters around the globe praying for us and ready to love us.

Although we have new abilities, a new heart, a new mind and a new spirit, we are still broken. The memory of the life we once lived, the choices we made, things we did that were against what God is are still fresh to us. Those things were what the Bible classifies as sin. Because those memories still reside in us, it creates new attractions to do those same things over and over again. Because it is what still feels comfortable to us. It is what still appeals to us because of the feelings that we associate with them. So even though sin no longer has power over our lives, it still holds an appeal and is why we still sin. It is why everyday a tough decision must be made to live how we once did or how the Holy Spirit enables us to live now. This is what Paul meant when he said that a struggle still rages within him. It is what many refer to as the battle between the old man and the new man.

As this battle rages, because the Holy Spirit now reigns in us we feel like complete failures. Which brings more familiar memories. Memories of not meeting the standards our parents, loved ones, friends set and feeling like we will lose their approval as a result. So we become harsh task masters on ourselves and others as we hold up standards we think they and us should be living by. So in effect, we become like harsh zoo keepers as we work to keep others and ourselves in well ordered, clean, cages. Cages formed from our need of approval from others. So we stop looking at ourselves under the light of God's passionate love for us but not only ourselves, but others as well. We end up relating to our brothers and sisters in Christ based on what they are doing and not doing, instead of God's amazing love and mercy.

Just as we do not have the ability to do what God requires or live to the character of God, which is always perfection, neither can they. When we keep these "brothers and sisters" at arms length instead of reaching out to them, we say more about ourselves than them. We say what we think about how God sees us, views us, and loves us. We will only be able to grasp the love and grace of God to the degree that we allow others to live in that same grace and love. Christ tells us in Matthew 7:1-3 that with the same judgment we use on others, we shall be judged. Romans 2:1 echoes this even further: "Some of you accuse others of doing wrong. But there is no excuse for what you do. When you judge others, you condemn yourselves, because you are guilty of doing the very same things."

It is not that we should condone sin or not challenge others to live according to who they are in Christ, but it is how we communicate this and what is the attitude of **our** heart. Most of the time we judge from a self-righteous, "let me show you what you are doing wrong" attitude. Take a few minutes and read these three passages that describe God's way of correction, which always involves love and **our** humility: Matthew 18:15-18, Hebrews 3:13, 1 Thessalonians 5:11.

Paul even brings another and possibly the greatest truth pertinent to the answer on how we live in relationships with our brothers and sisters in Christ or live as a part of the Body of Christ. It is the failure to get this passage that leads to many breaks in the Body, rifts in the family and separation. Often, when it comes to Galatians 6:1-3, many will point out how we should be carrying our brothers and sisters burdens. They will point out how Paul says that we should be letting our brothers know when they have stumbled or may be doing something that is wrong. Yet, often verse three is left out in that same passage.

This is the key verse to the other two. "For if anyone thinks he is something, when he is nothing, he deceives himself."

The first step towards relating to our brothers and sisters is humbling ourselves to realize we are nothing without Christ. We are the great nobodies, who have been made somebodies by the blood of Jesus. We have not one bit of ability to do what God wants to boast about. Not to mention that the reason why grace is a free gift is so that as Paul said, in Ephesians 2:9, "It isn't something you have earned, so there is nothing you can brag about." As a result not one of our brothers or sisters in Christ should ever be classified as fair game, because they do not measure up to our standards. The only way we can help our brothers and sisters in times of need is to become nobodies for Christ so that we might carry them when they cannot stand.

So, yes indeed we are part of the family of God, a bunch of nobodies who God has made somebodies, and as we live in that perspective we learn to treat others with the same grace and mercy that God gives to us every day.

Along with becoming part of a large family, we also have been adopted as sons of God (Romans 8:14-17, Galatians 4:5-6, Ephesians 1:5). As these verses so rightly point out, not only are we now sons of God, but we also have been given the ability to cry out, "Abba Father." That is like calling God, "Daddy." As God's children our inheritance is nothing less than the Kingdom of God, an eternal home with Him and no longer are we cast off (Ephesians 3:1, Hebrews 12:28).

What a blessed privilege to now be in God's family! Now let's live up to our identity!

Do I need to go to church?

Often Hebrews 10:24-25, which says that we should not neglect to come together and encourage each other, is used incorrectly to make people feel guilty if they are not in church every time the doors are opened. Those who have accepted Christ as their Savior **are** the Church, no matter where they are or happen to worship. The Church is not a building or an organization, but an organism, a living group of people who share common beliefs and one mind regarding Jesus Christ.

So a better way of looking at it might be that we do not go to church, but we gather with like-minded believers, our brothers and sisters in Christ. The Body can gather, worship, encourage and build one another up in many places and in many ways especially with today's internet.

Most believers in the western part of the world go to an actual physical building. But many believers in the Eastern blocks cannot gather for fear of persecution or do not have a building in which to gather. Then there are those who are shut in, in retirement homes, assisted living centers, handicapped, or do not have transportation, all of which may keep people from gathering in a physical location. "Africans never knew they were not worshiping or not doing church correctly until western missionaries came and told them '**Oh no!** You're doing this incorrectly, you must build a building and worship in it.'" – Doctor Howard Brown, World Prayr senior team member and missionary to Kenya for ten years.

While the above is true, the other error that often occurs is when we isolate ourselves and do not seek encouragement or to be with our brothers and sisters in Christ. It must be stressed that the Christian faith is not meant to be lived in isolation, nor are we to be separated from the rest of the Body. Hebrews 3:13 instructs, "But exhort one another every day, as long as it is called "today," that none of you may be hardened by the deceitfulness of sin." We truly are relational beings who grow, thrive and become more Christlike by being in relationships. Jody Neufeld, author of *Daily Devotions of Ordinary People – Extraordinary God* said, "Christ built His Church on people, not stones. He shared with the Samaritan woman where worship of God would happen and it wasn't a building."

So while we may worship and gather in many ways and forms, the point is we should be gathering so that we are being sharpened by other Christians. In choosing a local body of believers to meet with, we should seek one where God is kept as **the** focus, the Word of God is taught as the sole authority, the gospel of grace is preached, lived and emphasized consistently, all the gifts of the Body are in active use, spiritual discipline is happening and people are being baptized and partaking of the Lord's Supper. At the same time, the body of believers should be encouraging those who are a part of their local family to be coming together, getting to know each other, opening up to others about our common failures and reminding all, as they share their common failures, that God's grace is enough and He is deeply in love with us and we are the apple of His eye (Zechariah 2:8).

What is the best way to share my new faith?

At first, when we want to share our faith, we may feel over-whelmed as we may not know how exactly to do it or we feel somehow under-qualified. This is quite common, but the real problem is we do not yet know the Word of God. When we become more familiar with God's Word we will find ourselves more comfortable in sharing the truth of God's Word (2 Timothy 2:15). Peter said that "we should have an answer for every man who asks us of the hope that is in us" (1 Peter 3:15). There are three things that will help you as you share:

1) Briefly share your story of how you lived your life **before** you came to Christ. You will be surprised at the amount of people who will find your story easy to relate to.

2) Share what you **know** of God's Word, then trust God to do the rest. His Word always accomplishes **His** purposes, even if you do not see the results right away.

3) Remember that we are all cracked and broken vessels of God. None of us have the ability to know more of God's Word. We all have the same Holy Spirit teaching us God's Word. Because of gifts that God has given us it may be easier for others to share or teach God's Word. However, all of us have a responsibility to share God's Word. That is why we have been given the Holy Spirit, to enable us to be able to do so. Paul said in 2 Corinthians 12:9, "But he said to me, 'My grace is sufficient for you, for my power is made perfect in weakness. Therefore I will boast all the more gladly of my weaknesses, so that the power of Christ may rest upon me.'"

Keep in mind though that the people closest to us may not notice a big difference in our lives, and so they may not bother to listen. They see no reason to want what we have, since they see no difference. The greatest way to share our faith is to exhibit God's love to those God brings in our paths and into our lives. The greatest way to share God's love is often not in words but through a generous spirit, acts of kindness, not responding to how someone may have just treated us but with the grace God gives each of us new each day. Remember that it is important to pray before we share, after we share and for those we want to share with. Then realize it is **God's** job to bring them to Himself, while He only asks us to be willing to share our faith. We are not responsible if they do not accept (1 Corinthians 3:5-9).

How can I know God's will for my life?

This is the question of the decades. Even those who have been saved for a long time, still ask this question. It seems as though the answer is often out of reach.

Often, when we ask this question we are not looking for God's will, but for God to be a fortune teller. For surely God knows the future and if He will tell us, our lives will be better, easier, smoother, and more comfortable and we will fail less.

God is not interested in our being comfortable, self-sufficient, or our lives being easier at the expense of not doing or allowing those things which mold us into His image. He's interested in us becoming more who He designed us to be and dependent on Him. God will always bring situations in our lives that bring us to the point of utter desperation. As He brings us to this point we stop relying on our own strength and abilities to live this life. We then reach for His grace, given through the Holy Spirit, to live and make choices that are often foreign to us in order to reflect that we are loved by God. Sometimes the only light He will give us is what will illuminate the next step before us. This is why Psalm 119:105 says, "Your word is a lamp to my feet and a light to my path."

Trying to figure out what God wants from us is not that difficult. Just remember **His** ways are greater than our ways and **His** thoughts are higher than ours (Isaiah 55:8-9). So if God made it hard for us to find out what He wants from us, we never would discover it.

Here is what God wants:

- To love Him with all of our heart (Matthew 22:36-37).
- To love others as ourselves (Matthew 22:39).
- To offer our bodies as living sacrifices (Romans 12:1).
- To not be conformed to the ways of this world (Romans 12:2).
- To prefer others above ourselves (Romans 12:10).
- To not just consider your own things, but the things of others as well (Philippians 2:4).

- To bear your brothers' and sisters' burdens (Galatians 6:2).
- To be gentle and kind with each other (Ephesians 4:1-2).
- To Forgive Each other (Ephesians 4:31).
- To bear the fruits of the spirit (Galatians 5:16-26).
- To build one another up and encourage each other (Ephesians 4:29).
- To live according to our new selves (Ephesians 4:24).
- To work to provide for others (Ephesians 4:28).
- To not worry (Matthew 6:25-34).
- To lay up treasures in heaven (Matthew 6:19-21).
- To offer our bodies as instruments of righteousness (Romans 6).
- To serve as his ministers, instruments of His glory (1 Peter 1:9).
- To study the Word of God (2 Timothy 2:15).
- Do all things to His glory (1 Corinthians 10:31).
- To count all things loss but to know Him (Philippians 3:8).
- To walk humbly and love mercy (Micah 6:8).
- To be accountable one to another (James 5:16).

Christ said that those who follow Him must hate their lives for His sake. In saying this He was saying that we need to live in a way that we are not seeking our own desires and purposes in life but those desires and purposes that bring God honor, praise, and represent who He is. So consider this, there has never been a greater gift given to a bride than the gift of grace that cost the bridegroom everything. Reflecting on the price of that gift, the great agony Christ encountered in the garden, and the pain He endured through suffering and loss leads one to a deep heart of gratitude. This gratitude leads to a life in which deep passion and joy is found, not in seeking to impress God or anyone else with what we do, but to say thank you in worship of the father and in service to others. Given that, where such a life is not evident, it is not always an issue with our following what God wants us to do, but understanding our identity, and the price that was paid for the identity.

When we lose focus on our identity, being told to be more obedient, being given further instructions, being told what to do, stressing over becoming more pleasing to God, sweating out God's will, over worrying about whether we are holy enough or not, will not always correct the issue and in fact may make it worse. Instead we need to stop and reflect on the message and truth of the gospel. A gospel that tells us that even when we did not know we needed to be rescued, Christ came to rescue us from the wrath of God and eternal condemnation. In doing so He not only rescued us from the demands of a righteous and perfect God, He enabled us to come into a relationship with the One who created us. As we choose to remind ourselves of these truths moment by moment it will create within us a heart of gratitude and love. Love for the One who gave all, gave favor regardless of our response and now finds deep delight in us. As that love builds up inside of us it will come out of us into the lives of others. As it does we will reflect not only God's glory, but His love, mercy and grace.

As you walk on this journey we call grace, you may discover passions that bubble up inside of you. Explore them. As you explore them, you may find doors opening, the passion growing, people being reached for Christ, and you may just find the very thing you were designed for, what is often said to be our 'calling,' but what God identifies as our created purpose.

After following all these things we have discussed and allowing God, through the Holy Spirit working in us to remind us of the truths of not only the gospel but the word of God to make these things true in your life, whatever else you may find you desire to do — do it! Really — Wing It! Live life! Enjoy Life! Have a great adventure! Live as though you were dying, (because you are!) have nothing to lose, (because you don't!) and as a result — risk anything (because you can)! While God is never pleased with sin and in fact hates it, he has indeed opened the cages, set us free (Isaiah 61:1) to be wild for Him, adventurous, creative. For God takes ordinary people like us and through His extraordinary work enables us to live for Him in extraordinary ways. Just living for Him is being extraordinary in a day and age when the norm is anything but. It is through using ordinary folks, what the world often considers weak and using them for His purpose that He is indeed most glorified and that is never ordinary.

Truly you now need nothing and have everything you need to live this life as God intended (2 Peter 1:3). You can choose to serve and love others with no expectations and regardless of whether it is returned, for God is enough. We no longer need to allow the past to controls us with regrets or shame or feelings of failure or inadequacy, because God no longer condemns us for not meeting His standards, who cares what anyone else says (Romans 8:33-34). You can also live without the fear of rejection, for God will never reject you. So what or who else matters (Romans 5: 2). When you blow it, and you will, confess and accept the new grace and forgiveness God has waiting for you (1 John 1:9)! **WOW!** Now, take time and experience life as it was intended, in the worship of the Beloved and in total sacrifice for others. Rest comfortable in the assurance that **He** has got it and controls every molecule. Now that's **freedom!**

> The gospel of justifying faith means that while Christians are, in themselves still sinful and sinning, yet in Christ, in God's sight, they are accepted and righteous. So we can say that we are more wicked than we ever dared believe, but more loved and accepted in Christ than we ever dared hope — at the very same time. This creates a radical new dynamic for personal growth. It means that the more you see your own flaws and sins, the more precious, electrifying, and amazing God's grace appears to you. But on the other hand, the more aware you are of God's grace and acceptance in Christ, the more able you are to drop your denials and self-defenses and admit the true dimensions and character of your sin.[*]

---

[*] Timothy Keller, *Paul's Letter to the Galatians: Living in Line with the Truth of the Gospel*. Redeemer Presbyterian Church. 2003, p2

RESOURCES

We have created this wonderful list of resources for you of blogs, podcasts, authors, and books and recommend you use them to explore and further build your relationship with God on your walk of grace.

Print Books

Brown, Steve. *A Scandalous Freedom*. Howard Books. 2004.

_____. *Three Free Sins: God's Not Mad at You*. Howard Books. 2012.

_____, *What was I Thinking?: Things I've Learned Since I Knew It All*. Howard Books. Annotated Edition. 2006.

Campbell, James. *Broken*. PIP Printing. 2014.

Fitzpatrick, Elyse. *Because He Loves Me*. Crossway. 2010.

Forde, Gerhard. *On Being A Theologian Of The Cross*. Wm. B. Eerdmans Publishing Company. 1997.

_____. *Justification By Faith: A Matter Of Life and Death*. Wipf & Stock Publishing. Reprint Edition. 2012.

Havner, Vance. *Jesus Only*. F.H. Revell Company. 1969.

Holocomb, Justin. *On The Grace of God*. Crossway. First Edition. 2013.

Horton, Michael. *The Gospel Driven Life*. Baker Books. Reprint Edition. 2012.

_____. *The Christian Faith: Systematic Theology for Pilgrims on the Way*. Zondervan. 2011.

_____. *Putting Amazing Back into Grace: Embracing the Heart of the Gospel.* Baker Books. 2011.

Keller, Timothy. *Paul's Letter to the Galatians: Living in Line with the Truth of the Gospel.* Redeemer Presbyterian Church. 2003.

_____. *The Prodigal God.* Riverhead Trade. Reprint Edition. 2011.

_____. *Walking with God Through Pain and Suffering.* Dutton Adult. 2013.

_____. *The Reason for God: Belief in an Age of Skepticism.* Riverhead Trade. Reprint Edition. 2009.

_____. *The Freedom Of Self-Forgetfulness: The Path to true Christian Joy.* 10Publishing. 2012.

_____. *Every Good Endeavor : Connecting Your Work to God's Work.* Dutton Adult. 2012.

Manning, Brennan. *Ragamuffin Gospel.* Multnomah Books. 2005.

_____. *Abba's Child: The Cry of the Heart for Intimate Belonging.* NavPress. 2002.

_____. *Ruthless Trust: The Ragamuffin's Path to God.* HarperCollins. 2009.

Piper, John. *Don't Waste Your Life.* Crossway. First Edition. 2003.

_____. *Desiring God: Meditations of a Christian Hedonist.* The Doubleday Religious Publishing Group. 2011.

Platt, David. *Radical: Taking Back Your Faith from the American Dream.* Multnomah Books. 2010.

Tchividjian, Tullian. *Jesus + Nothing= Everything.* Crossway. 2011.

_____, (Blogpost) *The Gospel Coalition.* November 11, 2010, "Suffering Does Not Rob You Of Joy – Idolatry Does"

Tripp, Paul. *What Did You Expect: Redeeming the Realities of Marriage*. Crossway. 2012.

_____. *Dangerous Calling: Confronting the Unique Challenges of Pastoral Ministry*. Crossway. 2012.

Zahl, Paul. *Grace In Practice: A Theology of Everyday Life*. Wm.B. Eerdmans Publishing Company. 2007

Blogs

Beliefs Of The Heart http://beliefsoftheheart. com/

Christ Community Church - Scotty Smith - "Heavenward"

http://www.christcommunity.org/NewsResources/Blogs/tabid/93/articleType/AuthorView/authorID/332/scotty777. aspx

DASHHOUSE http://dashhouse.com/

dear ephesus http://dearephesus.com/

Desiring God http://www.desiringgod.org/

Dropping Keys http://dropping-keys.webs.com/

Energion Publications http://energion.com/discuss/ and http://jody.energion.com/

J.D. Greer http://www.jdgreear.com/my_weblog/2014/04/chosen-to-suffer.html

Jen Wilken http://jenwilkin.blogspot.com/

Key Life Ministries http://www.keylife.org/

Kim M Crandall http://kimmcrandall.com/

Liberate http://liberate.org/

MockingBird http://www.mbird.com/

Practical Theology For Women http://www.theologyforwomen.org/

The Heidelblog http://heidelblog.net/

World Prayr http://worldprayrblog.org

Podcasts and Audio Message Sites

Desiring God http://www.desiringgod.org/

Key Life Ministries http://www.keylife.org/

Learn Out Loud (Timothy Keller) http://www.learnoutloud.com/Podcast-Directory/Religion-and-Spirituality/Christian-Living/Timothy-Keller-Podcast/47658

Let My People Think, Just Thinking (Ravi Zacharias) http://www.rzim.org/podcasts/

Liberate http://liberate.org/

MockingBird http://www.mbird.com/

Paul Tripp http://paultripp.com/

Ransomed Heart Ministries (John Eldredge) http://www.ransomedheart.com/podcast

Revive Our Hearts (Nancy DeMoss) http://www.reviveourhearts.com/radio

The Alternative With Dr Tony Evans http://www.oneplace.com/ministries/the-alternative/subscribe/

The Briefing (Albert Mohler) http://www.albertmohler.com/category/the-briefing/

The Heidelblog http://heidelblog.net/

Voddie Baucham http://www.gracefamilybaptist.net/sermons/

White Horse Inn http://www.whitehorseinn.org/

World Prayr Podcast - aptly names SWEEETTTTTT Perf
 Grace. Where we bring you a collection of Pastors from
 around the web. You might really enjoy our Grace For The
 Moment which are short 3 to 9 minute podcasts every Mon-
 day and Friday.

Authors

Alcorn, Randy
Black, David Alan
Brown, Steve
Capon, Robert
Fitzpatrick, Elyse
Forde, Gerhard
Galli, Mark
Horton, Michael
Machen, James Greshem
Manning, Brennan
Neufeld, Henry
Tchividjian, Tullian
Thompson, Jessica
Tripp, Paul
Yancey, Phillip

We recommend most of what our publisher, *Energion
Publications*, prints, which is why we have developed a good relationship with them. Contact them as they would be happy to
steer you in the right path.

AFTERWORD

We pray this book from World Prayr blessed you. We hope that it has answered many of your questions. World Prayr really is working to "Reconnect a Broken World." We do this by offering prayer, God's word and encouraging thoughts to others online. We also do this by supporting other ministries and helping those who need to get connected to a local church.

Find out more about how World Prayr is working through social media, local churches and global ministries to build God's kingdom through our website
http://worldprayr.org/

We have a team of wonderful servants of God. This team diligently serves others in various ways, helping to pray for and encourage others in Christ. We would love to have you become a part of this wonderful team. If you would like to join our family in serving others around the globe, please fill out our form on our "Serve Beside Us" page.
http://worldprayr.org/servebesideus

Perhaps you have a need for prayer or just someone to talk to; we are waiting to do just that through our Reconnection Team. Contact us at needhelp@worlprayr.org. We have someone waiting to pray with you and work with you to connect with others who are waiting to serve you.

We guarantee you will be encouraged through our blog as we bring different writers from around the world who are both guests and teammates.
http://worldprayrblog.org/

Check out our podcasts where our founder and other pastors and ministry leaders share their thoughts. You may really enjoy our *Grace for the Moments* podcast on Mondays and Fridays. These are quick thoughts on passages of God's Word. Each one is no more than nine minutes and most are less than five. Yet, each one packs a powerful, grace themed message.

http://www.worldprayr.org/GraceThatsTight/

You can also follow us on our social media accounts where you may receive daily encouragement in your walk of grace.

Twitter - https://twitter.com/WorldPrayr

Facebook - https://www.facebook.com/worldprayrinc

Google+ - https://plus.google.com/u/0/b/118353923097000 741532/+WorldprayrOrg2009/posts

Pinterest - http://www.pinterest.com/faithfactr/

YouTube - https://www.youtube.com/worldprayr

Currently Working On and Coming Soon!

Imagine being able to shop at a combination of Kohl's and a Christian Bookstore. Then, not only be able to shop at such a store, but when you were done shopping being asked who you would like to give 100% of the profit to. Now, why is that a radical concept? It is because there is not another store in existence like it; not online or off. World Prayr is working to release FaithFactr, a new concept in shopping. With its strong Shop-And-Donate message, it is the hope of all involved that FaithFactr will be a powerful tool to help churches and ministries in their mission to build God's kingdom.

http://faithfactr.com/

What we are also Working On!

World Prayr, along with EvanTell Ministry (http://www.evan-tell.org) and Deep Blue Marketing (http://deepbluemarketing.com), are in the process of developing a one-of-a-kind app. Imagine having at your fingertips an app that will help you to not only give the gospel to someone, but to talk with those involved in various cults.

Also, imagine being able to answer questions on how to walk in grace with someone. Now imagine too, being able to record and list your prayer requests so others can pray for them. Does that sound like a unique one of a kind app? It is! Does that sound like a large project? It is! Stay Tuned!

CPSIA information can be obtained
at www.ICGtesting.com
Printed in the USA
FSOW01n2304290615
8382FS